Best Easy Day Hikes
Santa Barbara

D0089163

Help Us Keep This Guide Up to Date

Every effort has been made by the author and editors to make this guide as accurate and useful as possible. However, many things can change after a guide is published—trails are rerouted, regulations change, facilities come under new management, etc.

We would love to hear from you concerning your experiences with this guide and how you feel it could be improved and kept up to date. While we may not be able to respond to all comments and suggestions, we'll take them to heart and we'll also make certain to share them with the author. Please send your comments and suggestions to the following address:

Globe Pequot Press
Reader Response/Editorial Department
P.O. Box 480
Guilford, CT 06437

Or you may e-mail us at:

editorial@GlobePequot.com

Thanks for your input, and happy trails!

Best Easy Day Hikes Series

Best Easy Day Hikes
Santa Barbara

Bryn Fox

FALCONGUIDES

GUILFORD, CONNECTICUT
HELENA, MONTANA

AN IMPRINT OF GLOBE PEQUOT PRESS

To buy books in quantity for corporate use
or incentives, call **(800) 962–0973**
or e-mail **premiums@GlobePequot.com**.

FALCONGUIDES®

Copyright © 2009 by Morris Book Publishing, LLC

ALL RIGHTS RESERVED. No part of this book may be reproduced or transmitted in any form by any means, electronic or mechanical, including photocopying and recording, or by any information storage and retrieval system, except as may be expressly permitted in writing from the publisher. Requests for permission should be addressed to Globe Pequot Press, Attn: Rights and Permissions Department, P.O. Box 480, Guilford, CT 06437.

Falcon, FalconGuides, and Outfit Your Mind are registered trademarks of Morris Book Publishing, LLC.

TOPO! Explorer software and SuperQuad source maps courtesy of National Geographic Maps. For information about TOPO! Explorer, TOPO!, and Nat Geo Maps products, go to www.topo.com or www .natgeomaps.com.

Maps by OffRoute Inc. © Morris Book Publishing, LLC

Library of Congress Cataloging-in-Publication Data is available on file.

ISBN 978-0-7627-5117-4

Printed in the United States of America

10 9 8 7 6 5 4 3 2 1

The author and Globe Pequot Press assume no liability for accidents happening to, or injuries sustained by, readers who engage in the activities described in this book.

Contents

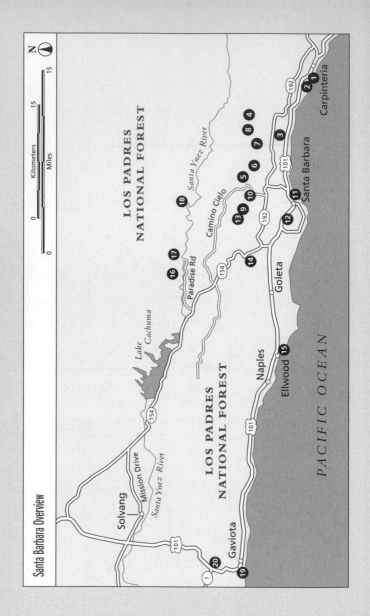

Santa Barbara Overview

Acknowledgments

Many thanks to all my hiking buddies—Jenny, Jannine, Josephine, Kira, and Alexa—who made logging the many miles it took to write this book even more entertaining. Thanks to Kerry at the Forest Service, the folks at the Channel Coast Chapter of the California State Parks, and the Montecito Trails Foundation for their intimate knowledge of the trails that they shared with me. Most of all, thanks to my incredibly supportive and understanding husband, Ben, who has accompanied me on many, many (many, many) miles and adventures throughout the writing of this book and throughout life.

Introduction

It is no surprise that in a city where the temperature rarely dips below 60 degrees any day of the year, locals and visitors alike tend to spend a lot of time outdoors in Santa Barbara. Just minutes from town is the Los Padres National Forest, which covers almost two million acres of land and stretches more than 220 miles from the northern end of Los Angeles County all the way up the coast to Big Sur. With more than 1,200 miles of trails traversing the park, there are potentially hundreds of options for day hiking and backpacking trips just moments from downtown and the beach. It would not be a difficult feat to have the epitome of a Santa Barbara day—spending a morning at the beach followed by an afternoon in the mountains.

The hardest thing about hiking in Santa Barbara is likely not finding a place to hike but narrowing down the options. In this book you will find twenty hikes, all within a short drive of town. Most hikes can be reached in less than fifteen minutes from downtown, with a few additional options a short ways up or down the coast in either direction. And every hike in this book can be done in a few hours or less. Each hike was handpicked in order to provide you with twenty options for hiking the Santa Barbara foothills where you'll get the most bang for your buck—the greatest scenery and the best escape to nature, all in a neat little package that hard-core outdoors enthusiasts and children alike can all enjoy. Even if you have limited time or limited abilities, you can do just about every hike in this book and still be back at the beach in time to watch the sunset.

Weather

You can hike every trail in this book every month of the year. Temperatures are mild year-round, ranging from highs in the low 60s in January to the high 70s in August, making for comfortable hiking temperatures in every season.

Rain does affect this area and can make some hikes up slippery canyons dangerous. It is also possible that rainfall can make the hikes listed off Paradise Road inaccessible if the Santa Ynez River rises high enough to close the road. This does happen from time to time, so if you are planning a hike up this way shortly after a heavy rain, it is a good idea to call the Forest Service before driving up to the trailhead. Most likely to be closed is the Red Rocks, which requires many creek crossings to reach the trailhead. January and February are the wettest months, with the monthly average rainfall at a whopping 4.7 inches.

More of a concern than rainfall is the threat of eternal sunshine. Many of the hikes in this area are relatively exposed, with sparse tree cover providing only rare moments of refuge from the sun. Though the temperature in town may only be in the 70s, the heat up on the hillside can feel much more intense; always bring plenty of water along. Don't forget extra for your four-legged friends if they will be joining you.

Wildfires have been a problem here in the past few years so it is always a good idea to check the status of the trails before heading out to the trailhead.

Wilderness Restrictions

Most of the hikes covered in this book are under the jurisdiction of the National Forest Service as part of the Los Padres National Forest. A few trails mentioned are actually within city or county parks, and a few are within the California state park system.

Some trails begin within a city or state park and then join a trail leading into Forest Service land. Each of these governing bodies has its own set of rules, so it is a good idea to become familiar with them. Perhaps the most significant difference are the laws pertaining to canine use. Within the city, dogs must be leashed. However, on Forest Service land dogs must simply be "under control at all times." This means that off-leash dogs are permitted; however if they are running wild and knocking into other hikers, you could very well be cited and fined. Because most hikes in this book begin from a trailhead that is technically on city or county property and you are likely parking on a city or county street, it is a good rule of thumb to keep your dog on a leash until you are a good quarter mile up the trail before letting him loose. The hike summaries will note when dogs are prohibited or are permitted only on a leash.

Any of the hikes listed in this book that begin by driving up CA 154 require that you purchase an Adventure Pass before parking, hiking, or doing just about anything. The Adventure Pass (per vehicle) can be purchased at the Los Prietos Ranger Station or from camp hosts at various campgrounds in the area. Often you will find volunteers simply wandering on foot, ready to sell you an Adventure Pass if you even look like you may be planning on stopping in the area. Don't ignore these folks—you will get a ticket if your car is spotted parked without a pass! In the end your fee goes to a good cause, so if you are going to enjoy the area, pay up.

Safety

The foothills of the Los Padres National Forest and other areas in this book are all relatively tame ways to spend an afternoon. However, like with all outdoor pursuits, a bit of knowledge and a few extra minutes of preparation can make hiking in this area far more enjoyable, not to mention safer.

Fires

Because of the significant lack of rainfall here, forest fires are a serious threat almost year-round but especially in late summer and early fall, also known as fire season. Campfires are permitted only in designated fire rings. At various times throughout the year, the Forest Service may prohibit fires altogether if the fire danger is extremely high.

Never build a fire outside a fire ring—no matter how desperate you are for a s'more. And always make sure your fire is completely out before leaving the site. Massive fires with tragic results can and have occurred because of campfires that were not properly extinguished.

Wildlife

Most wildlife you run into on these hikes will likely be harmless—lizards, nonpoisonous snakes, or perhaps rabbits. However, rattlesnakes, mountain lions, and even bears can be encountered.

- **Rattlesnakes** are the only kind of snake you might see out here that poses any real danger. They are most commonly seen in the warmest months, when they may be sunning themselves on warm rocks. If you see a rattlesnake, pass it at a distance if it is sitting still or patiently allow it to pass if you see it on the move.

You may want to use a walking stick when traveling in rocky or bushy areas to help notify any snakes of your presence. The most dangerous kind of rattlesnake is one that is startled.

- **Mountain lions** are rare, though they are seen from time to time. If there has been a recent mountain lion sighting on the trail you are hiking, there often will be a notice posted at the trailhead to beware. If you do encounter a mountain lion, the Forest Service advises that you do not attempt to run past it. Back away slowly while making yourself appear as large and aggressive as possible. If you pick up a small child that is with you, do not crouch down to do so.

- **Bears** are also rare in this area; however, there are many black bears within the forest. If you come across a bear, do not run. Keep your distance and try talking to the bear in a normal voice. Make yourself seen and heard, and let the bear recognize that you are not a threat as you back away slowly.

Noxious Plants

Perhaps the biggest threat to hikers in this area is poison oak, which can be found along many area trails, as well as along rivers and creeks and at parks and campgrounds. Poison oak can be especially daunting in the winter months when the stems are bare, making the plant much harder to identify. Familiarize yourself with what poison oak looks like before you head out, and avoid it as best you can.

A poison oak rash can take many days to appear, so if you even suspect that you have come into contact with the plant, wash up with cold running water as soon as possible. There are various products on the market made for removing the irritating oils off your skin. Tecnu and Zanfel are developed for this purpose and can be purchased at any drugstore. If you think you hiked through some poison oak, these products are well worth the investment.

Zero Impact

Trails in the Santa Barbara area are heavily used year-round. We, as trail users and advocates, must be especially vigilant to make sure our passage leaves no lasting mark. Here are some basic guidelines for preserving trails in the region:

- Pack out all your own trash, including biodegradable items like orange peels. You might also pack out garbage left by less considerate hikers.

- Don't approach or feed any wild creatures—the ground squirrel eyeing your snack food is best able to survive if it remains self-reliant.

- Don't pick wildflowers or gather rocks, antlers, feathers, and other treasures along the trail. Removing these items will only take away from the next hiker's experience.

- Avoid damaging trailside soils and plants by remaining on the established route. This is also a good rule of thumb for avoiding poison oak and stinging nettle, common regional trailside irritants.

- Don't cut switchbacks, which can promote erosion.

- Be courteous by not making loud noises while hiking.

- Many of these trails are multiuse, which means you'll share them with other hikers, trail runners, mountain bikers, and equestrians. Familiarize yourself with the proper trail etiquette, yielding the trail when appropriate.

- Use outhouses at trailheads or along the trail.

How to Use This Guide

This guide is designed to be simple and easy to use. Each hike is described with a map and summary information that delivers the trail's vital statistics: distance and type of hike (loop, lollipop, or out and back), approximate hiking time, difficulty, trail surface, best season for the hike, other trail users, canine compatibility, fees and permits, park schedule, relevant U.S. Geological Survey (USGS) maps, and trail contacts. Directions to the trailhead are also provided, along with a general description of what you'll see along the way. A detailed route finder (Miles and Directions) sets forth mileages between significant landmarks along the trail.

Hike Selection

The hikes listed in this book range from leisurely strolls to more challenging hikes. You will find hikes that range in distance from 1 mile to 6 miles and across varying terrain. Whether you are visiting for a weekend or a local of many years, you should find a hike in this book to serve your interests. There are excellent options for getting a good workout, as well as options that are best for days when you just want to get outside without too much effort. It is important to remember that while we believe these are the best easy day hikes in the area, not every hike is right for every person. Be sure to check out the Trail Finder to help you choose the right hike for you and your hiking partners.

Difficulty Ratings

These are all easy hikes, but easy is a relative term. Beginning at sea level, hiking into the mountains often, obviously, requires some elevation gain and hence, uphill climbing. To aid in selecting a hike that suits particular needs and abilities, each is rated easy, moderate, or more challenging. Bear in mind that even the most challenging routes can be made easy by hiking within your limits and taking rests when you need them.

- **Easy** hikes are generally short and flat, usually taking no more than an hour to complete.

- **Moderate** hikes involve some elevation gain and may require slightly more coordination than the easy hikes, often crossing streams or scrambling over rocks.

- **More challenging** hikes feature some steep stretches and greater distances and generally require more fitness and technical skills.

These are completely subjective ratings—consider that what you think is easy is entirely dependent on your level of fitness and coordination and the adequacy of your gear. If you are hiking with a group, you should select a hike with a rating that's appropriate for the least fit and prepared in your party.

Approximate hiking times are based on the assumption that on flat ground, most walkers average 2 to 3 miles per hour. Adjust that rate by the steepness of the terrain and your level of fitness (subtract time if you're an aerobic animal and add time if you're hiking with kids) and you have a ballpark hiking duration. Be sure to add more time if you plan to picnic or take part in other activities like bird watching or photography. It is also important to note that a hiking trip does not only entail moving time. Plan more time if you tend to take a lot of pictures or stop to frequently enjoy the views.

Trail Finder

Best Hikes for Beach/Coast Lovers
  1   Tar Pits/Carpinteria Bluffs
  11   Santa Barbara Waterfront
  12   Douglas Family Preserve
  15   Ellwood Bluffs/Butterfly Preserve

Best Hikes for Waterfalls
  5   Tangerine Falls
  8   San Ysidro Falls

Best Hikes for Children (aka the easiest of the easy)
  1   Tar Pits/Carpinteria Bluffs
  2   Carpinteria Salt Marsh
  3   Ennisbrook Trail
  12   Douglas Family Preserve
  14   San Antonio Creek Trail
  15   Ellwood Bluffs/Butterfly Preserve
  17   Lower Oso Trail

Best Hikes for Swimming Holes
  5   Tangerine Falls
  6   Cold Spring Trail: East Fork
  8   San Ysidro Falls
  18   Red Rocks

Best Hikes for Great Views
  4   Romero Canyon Loop
  7   McMenemy Hike
  9   Inspiration Point
  16   Aliso Canyon Loop
  19   Beach to Backcountry Trail

Map Legend

══⟨101⟩══	US Highway
══⟨225⟩══	State Highway
═══════	Local Road
= = = = = =	Unpaved Road
■■■■■■■■	Featured Route
- - - - - - - -	Trail
┼─┼─┼─┼─┼	Railroad
～～～	River/Creek
─··─··─	Intermittent Stream
⌂⌂	Marsh/Swamp
⬭	Ocean/Lake
⛲	Bench
▲	Campground
⌒	Cave
•—•	Gate
🅿	Parking
⊞	Picnic Area
■	Point of Interest/Structure
🚻	Restroom
○	Town
➓	Trailhead
⧉	Viewpoint/Overlook
⋙	Waterfall

1 Tar Pits/Carpinteria Bluffs

This blufftop hike traverses flat wooded trails directly above the beach. You'll pass a harbor seal rookery where you can stop and watch the seals before heading onto a peaceful tree-lined path with stunning views of the Pacific Ocean below.

Distance: 2.2 miles out and back

Approximate hiking time: 1 hour

Difficulty: Easy; mostly flat, smooth terrain

Trail surface: Dirt path

Best season: Year-round; seal pupping season from December to March

Other trail users: Joggers, occasional cyclists

Canine compatibility: Leashed dogs permitted

Fees and permits: No fees or permits required

Schedule: Anytime

Maps: USGS Carpinteria and White Ledge Peak

Trail contacts: Citizens of Carpinteria Bluffs; (805) 684-3712 City of Carpinteria Parks Department; (805) 684-5405

Finding the trailhead: From downtown Santa Barbara drive south on US 101 approximately 10 miles to the town of Carpinteria. Exit at Linden Avenue and turn right. Go 0.12 mile and turn left onto Carpinteria Avenue. Go 0.56 mile and turn right onto Arbol Verde Street. Take an immediate right on Concha Loma Drive. Go 0.1 mile and turn left onto Calle Ocho. Drive 0.2 mile until the road dead-ends. Park on the side of the road and walk across the train tracks. GPS: N34 23.315' / W119 30.807'

The Hike

The grassy overlook at the end of Calle Ocho is an excellent lookout point before you begin your hike. A set of stairs leads you down to the beach, where you can explore

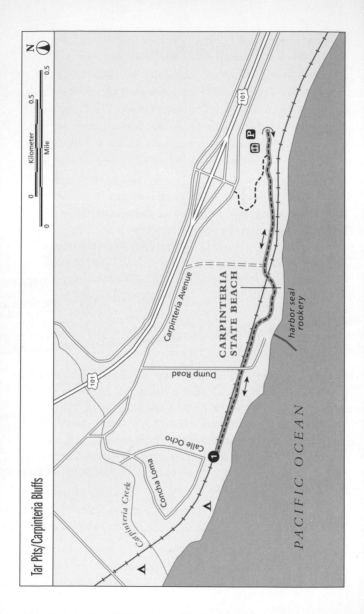

Tar Pits/Carpinteria Bluffs

N

Kilometer
0   0.5

Mile
0   0.5

Carpinteria Creek

Concha Loma

101

Calle Ocho

Dump Road

Carpinteria Avenue

CARPINTERIA
STATE BEACH

harbor seal
rookery

P

101

PACIFIC OCEAN

tidepools and see tar bubbling up through the surface of the sand—hence the name of the area. Thanks to the excellent waterproofing qualities of tar, when the Chumash Indians first came to this area, they used this particular spot to build boats. They nicknamed this spot Carpinteria, Spanish for "carpentry shop," which is now the name of the city. Get a little sand between your toes, and then begin your hike back up top by taking the wide path on the left of the grassy area.

Start by walking east. After 0.2 mile the trail becomes a dirt path that crosses a driveway. On your right is a pier that is used to service and supply the oil rigs that sit a few miles out to sea. Continue straight down this path. At 0.4 mile, just before the path dead-ends, there is a smaller trail on your right that connects Tar Pits Park and the Carpinteria Bluffs Nature Preserve. Take this trail and head southeast toward the ocean. At 0.5 mile the trail curves to the left. Right at this bend in the trail is a harbor seal rookery; one of only four in southern California and the only harbor seal rookery that is open to the public. Have a seat on the bench here to enjoy the show—best during the pupping season, December through March.

Past the seal rookery there are amazing views all along this stretch of trail, where on a clear day you can see the Channel Islands. Continue on until you reach a small fork at 0.6 mile. Stay to the left and cross the railroad tracks. On the other side of the tracks, you will see a small trail that heads straight and two wider trails that go right. Take the wide path on the far right to enter the Carpinteria Bluffs preserve.

The nature preserve is the result of many decades of advocacy from the residents of Carpinteria. Their efforts to preserve this land were finally realized in 1998, when an assortment of community environmental organizations closed escrow on the fifty-two-acre property, assuring it permanent protected status. The bluffs are now owned and managed by the City of Carpinteria while an easement held by the Land Trust for Santa Barbara County ensures that the land will never be developed by the city.

Follow the walkway lined with eucalyptus trees until it ends at 1.1 miles at the end of the preserve. On your left is a baseball field with public restrooms; to your right are sweeping views of the California coast. From here retrace your steps back to your car. Or you can continue to explore any of the smaller trails that offshoot the main trail. It is nearly impossible to get lost here if you remember to simply follow the coastline.

Miles and Directions

0.0 Start at the grassy overlook just beyond the railroad tracks. Take the wide dirt path on your left and head east.

0.2 Stay straight on the dirt path as it crosses a driveway.

0.4 Just past the sign for the harbor seal rookery, take the smaller trail on your right that heads toward the ocean.

0.5 Follow the trail as it curves left at the seal rookery.

0.6 Take the left fork and cross the railroad tracks again.

0.7 After the railroad tracks, turn right and take the wide path to the right of the eucalyptus grove.

1.1 Arrive at your turnaround point at the end of the Carpinteria Bluffs Nature Preserve. Retrace your steps.

2.2 Arrive back at the grassy overlook and walk across the railroad tracks to your car.

2 Carpinteria Salt Marsh

This nature walk travels through a 230–acre salt marsh. As one of the last remaining coastal estuaries in California, this thriving ecosystem is home to a variety of native plants, animals, and sea life. At the start of your walk, you will find yourself just a stone's throw away from a strip of beach that touts itself as the safest swimming beach in the world.

Distance: 1.2 miles out and back

Approximate hiking time: 1 hour

Difficulty: Easy; flat terrain, well-groomed path, and easy-to-follow trail

Hiking surface: Dirt path

Best season: Year-round

Other trail users: None

Canine compatibility: Dogs prohibited

Fees and permits: No fees or permits required

Schedule: Sunrise to sunset

Maps: USGS Carpinteria

Trail contacts: City of Carpinteria Parks and Recreation Department; (805) 684-5405

Finding the trailhead: From downtown Santa Barbara drive south on US 101 to Carpinteria. Exit at Linden Avenue and turn right, toward the beach. Drive 0.6 mile and turn right onto Sandyland Road. Drive 0.25 mile until the road ends at Ash Avenue. Park in the parking spots along Ash Avenue. GPS: N34 23.740' / W119 31.699'

The Hike

The Carpinteria salt marsh is one of the last remaining coastal estuaries in California. This unique wetland, where salt water and fresh water meet, yields ideal conditions for certain plants and animals. More than 190 species of birds, 37 species of fish, and 11 species of mammals have been observed here.

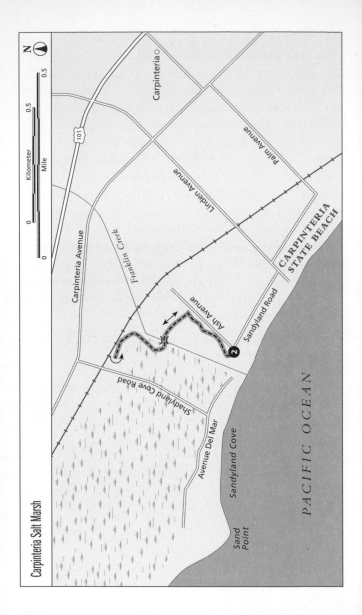

Carpinteria Salt Marsh

N

Kilometer
0   0.5

Mile
0   0.5

Carpinteria

Carpinteria Avenue

Franklin Creek

Linden Avenue

Palm Avenue

101

Shadyland Cove Road

Ash Avenue

Sandyland Road

CARPINTERIA STATE BEACH

Avenue Del Mar

Sandyland Cove

Sand Point

PACIFIC OCEAN

2

Threatened by nearby home construction, railroad tracks, and freeways, the 230-acre property has been a work in progress over the years. In 1977 the University of California National Reserve System purchased a portion of the marsh from eleven families living on adjacent properties and the acreage officially became the Salt Marsh Reserve. In the late 1990s, the University of California National Reserve System partnered with the Land Trust for Santa Barbara County, the State Coastal Conservancy, and the City of Carpinteria to purchase much of the remaining wetlands. Ninety percent of the salt marsh is now protected. In 1997 the park opened to the public, complete with convenient walking trails, a small amphitheater for classes, and informative interpretive signs posted along the trails.

You can begin this hike at any of the trailheads along Ash Avenue. To walk through the entire preserve, start at the trailhead closest to the beach. Walk into the preserve and follow the trail to the right. There are a few places along the way where you can take short detours farther into the wetlands.

Continue along the path as it skirts the perimeter of the estuary. This portion of the marsh is considered a Carpinteria City Park. You will pass a mobile home park on your right and then at 0.3 mile cross a small bridge. Once across, follow the path to your right. This land here on the far side of the bridge is owned in fee by the Land Trust for Santa Barbara County. At 0.6 mile the trail ends at a small paved circle. Turn around here and retrace your steps back to the trailhead.

Miles and Directions

0.0 Start at the trailhead on Ash Avenue and follow it to the right.

0.3 Cross the bridge and find the trail again on the right side.

0.6 The trail dead-ends at a paved spiral. Turn around and retrace your steps to the trailhead.

1.2 Arrive back at the trailhead.

3 Ennisbrook Trail

From the heart of Montecito, this flat nature walk is a brief stroll through history. Across old stone bridges and along a butterfly preserve, you can meander along the oaks, taking brief trips through the exclusive Ennisbrook neighborhood. An excellent spot for bird-watchers, here you can see warbling vireos and Pacific Slope flycatchers.

Distance: 1.8-mile lollipop

Approximate hiking time: 1 hour

Difficulty: Easy; flat surface and easy-to-follow path

Trail surface: Dirt trail and paved path

Best season: Year-round

Other trail users: Equestrians, joggers

Canine compatibility: Leashed dogs permitted

Fees and permits: No fees or permits required

Schedule: Anytime

Maps: USGS Carpinteria

Trail contacts: Montecito Trails Foundation; (805) 568-0833

Finding the trailhead: From downtown Santa Barbara take US 101 south toward Montecito. Exit at San Ysidro Road. Turn left onto San Ysidro Road and drive 1 block to San Leandro Lane. Turn right and follow San Leandro 0.26 mile to a fork in the road where San Leandro turns to the left. Turn left and continue 0.1 mile. Turn right onto San Leandro again. (The name of the street is the same, although the road actually takes two sharp turns.) Continue 0.2 mile and park along the side of the road in front of the white picket fence. GPS: N34 25.533' / W119 37.322'

The Hike

Nestled amidst the sprawling mansions of Montecito, you might be surprised to find a hiking trail, let alone a hiking

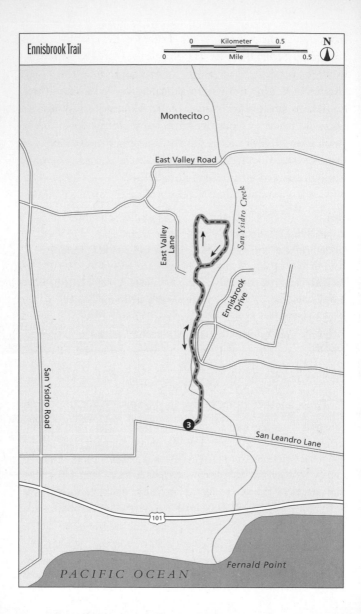

Kilometer

Mile

N

Montecito

East Valley Road

San Ysidro Creek

East Valley Lane

Ennisbrook Drive

San Ysidro Road

3

San Leandro Lane

101

PACIFIC OCEAN

Fernald Point

trail open to the general public. Formerly the center of polo culture in Santa Barbara, the Ennisbrook area was bought in 1986 to be developed for the first time since the Great Depression. The new owner's plan to build sixty-three homes on the property was approved under a condition: Forty-four acres of the property would be made available to the public in the form of a nature preserve. In 1997 the Land Trust for Santa Barbara County accepted an easement through the property, granting protected status to the area. Now a large population of local birds and monarch butterflies call this area home.

Begin this hike by walking through the white gate, past a small green building. After a few yards pass over San Ysidro Creek on an old stone bridge. Turn left after crossing the creek to enter the preserve. At 0.2 mile the looming houses across the road will remind you that you are in fact in the middle of town. The dirt path then becomes a paved sidewalk and leads you out to a road. Once on the road, continue straight ahead. After 0.1 mile the trail picks back up on the left side of the road and once again drops down toward the creek and away from the street.

Cross another stone bridge at 0.5 mile. After the bridge you will see a fork. Continue straight to head out toward the far end of the reserve. Shortly after the fork the trail spits you out onto a cul-de-sac on East Valley Lane. Look for the trail on the right side of the street; continue on this trail, following the curves of the road. At 0.8 mile the trail turns right and heads back into the trees. At 0.9 mile there is a small fork. Turn right to begin a small loop. Cross over the creek at 1.1 miles and find yourself at a fork where you can get back on the trail you originally started on. Turn left once you reach this main trail, and head back the way you came.

Miles and Directions

0.0   Begin at the white picket fence on San Leandro Lane. Walk through the gate and straight down the path. Cross over the stone bridge and turn left.

0.2   Continue straight ahead on the trail as it becomes a paved path.

0.3   The trail intersects Ennisbrook Drive. Turn left to continue up the road.

0.4   Find the trail on the left side of the road. Here it drops back down toward the creek, away from the road.

0.5   Cross the stone bridge on your left.

0.6   Arrive at a fork and continue straight. (FYI: The trail to your right is the trail you will return on.)

0.7   Arrive at the cul-de-sac at the end of East Valley Lane. Find the trail on your right, following along the road.

0.8   The trail turns sharply to the right, back into the trees and away from the road.

0.9   Turn right at the fork.

1.1   Cross over the creek again. Once across, come to another fork. Turn left and continue back toward the trailhead.

1.8   Arrive back at the trailhead.

4 Romero Canyon Loop

This favorite local route begins with a short trip up a dirt access road before heading off the main trail onto a shaded singletrack. Follow the creek for a 2-mile uphill workout before merging back with the dirt road and returning on a long, meandering downhill with panoramic views of the Pacific.

Distance: 6.0-mile loop
Approximate hiking time: 1.5 to 2.5 hours
Difficulty: Moderate; steep uphill sections
Trail surface: Dirt road and forested trail
Best season: Year-round
Other trail users: Mountain bikers

Canine compatibility: Dogs permitted
Fees and permits: No fees or permits required
Schedule: Anytime
Maps: USGS Carpinteria
Trail contacts: USDA Forest Service, Los Padres National Forest; (805) 967-3481; Montecito Trails Foundation; (805) 568-0833

Finding the trailhead: From downtown Santa Barbara drive south on US 101. Exit at Sheffield Drive. Turn left off the exit and then make an immediate right onto Sheffield Drive. Drive 1.3 miles to East Valley Road. Turn left onto East Valley Road and then make an immediate right onto Romero Drive. Follow Romero Drive as it twists and turns its way up into the Montecito foothills. Drive 1.3 miles and turn right onto Bella Vista Drive. Drive 0.3 mile to the trailhead at the bend in the road on Bella Vista Drive. Park alongside the road; the trailhead is on your left. GPS: N34 27.177' / W119 35.444'

The Hike

Initially developed by the Chumash Indians as a means of obtaining food and trade from over the mountain in the

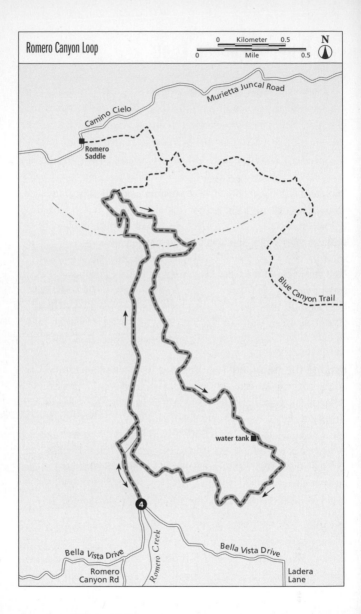

Romero Canyon Loop

Kilometer
0   0.5
Mile
0   0.5

N

Murietta Juncal Road

Camino Cielo

Romero
Saddle

Blue Canyon Trail

water tank

4

Bella Vista Drive

Bella Vista Drive

Romero
Canyon Rd

Romero Creek

Ladera
Lane

Santa Ynez Valley, the Romero Canyon Trail currently encompasses both a singletrack trail that follows the creek and a wide, flat, dirt access road that winds through the canyon above the creek. In 1933 the Civil Conservation Corps bulldozed the entire road in order to service a dam above. The road fell into disrepair in the mid 1960s, only to have the lower portion bulldozed again (to the dismay of some who enjoyed the singletrack), most recently in 2007 to better fight the Zaca wildfire.

You can hike this canyon by starting up the dirt road and turning around at any point. Or you can make it a loop, as described here, by branching off the main road to hike up the creek and then merge with the road for the trip back.

To hike the loop, begin at the trailhead on Bella Vista Drive and head northwest. After two creek crossings, make a left turn at 0.7 mile where a sign simply says TRAIL. Turn left and follow the switchbacks toward the creek. Continue straight on the trail as you cross the creek many times. At 1.3 miles there are nice cascades and an excellent shady spot to sit. California bay trees line the hike here. The leaves can be picked and used for cooking as seasoning in soups and curries. Just remember to take the leaf out before eating— bay leaves are bitter to bite into.

Continue straight and cross the creek two more times before eventually reaching the top of the trail where it inter-sects Romero Canyon Road and the trail leading to Blue Canyon. There is a confusing plethora of signs here that all simply say TRAIL, each pointing in different directions. Take the trail on your right to head back down on Romero Canyon Road.

At 2.6 miles pass the creek as it flows over a paved spot on the trail. Continue straight on this trail as it winds down,

dipping in and out of the canyon for surprisingly pictur-
esque views around every bend. Continue straight ahead.
At 5.3 miles you will see the trail you hiked up on your
right. Continue straight and return the way you came back
to the trailhead.

Miles and Directions

0.0 Start hiking northwest from the trailhead.

0.3 Continue straight on the dirt road.

0.4 Cross the creek and continue straight.

0.7 Take the small trail on your left, marked TRAIL.

0.8 Continue straight ahead. (FYI: A small trail on your left takes
you to the creek.)

1.0 Cross the creek and continue straight ahead.

1.4 Cross the creek and continue straight ahead.

1.9 Reach a four-way trail junction. Take the fork on your right to
continue on Romero Canyon Road.

4.1 Arrive at a junction with a trail on your left, with a locked
gate at the entrance. Continue straight down Romero Canyon Road.

5.3 Continue straight ahead on the road. Cross the creek.

6.0 Arrive back at the trailhead.

5 Tangerine Falls

Beginning at the Cold Spring trailhead, this hike travels the west fork of the creek for a ways before branching off the main trail and following the middle fork. You will rock hop and climb your way up the creek past pools and cascades before arriving at the gorgeous 200-foot waterfall.

Distance: 2.2 miles out and back
Approximate hiking time: 2 hours
Difficulty: More challenging; technical rock scramble at the end
Trail surface: Dirt trail
Best season: Year-round
Other trail users: Backpackers
Canine compatibility: Dogs permitted

Fees and permits: No fees or permits required
Schedule: Anytime
Maps: USGS Carpinteria
Trail contacts: USDA Forest Service, Los Padres National Forest; (805) 967-3481; Montecito Trails Foundation; (805) 568-0833

Finding the trailhead: From Santa Barbara take US 101 south toward Montecito. Exit at Hot Springs Road and turn left. Go 2.2 miles and turn left onto East Mountain Drive. Go 1.1 miles to a bend in the road where the creek runs across it. Park along the road on either side of the creek. GPS: N34 27.353' / W119 39.176'

The Hike

Tangerine Falls is perhaps the most spectacular waterfall in the area. Almost 200 feet tall, the falls can be especially impressive after a big rain. The falls sits at the end of the middle fork of the Cold Spring Trail, which was the original route of the Cold Spring Road when it was used for traveling over the mountain. Although the site of the

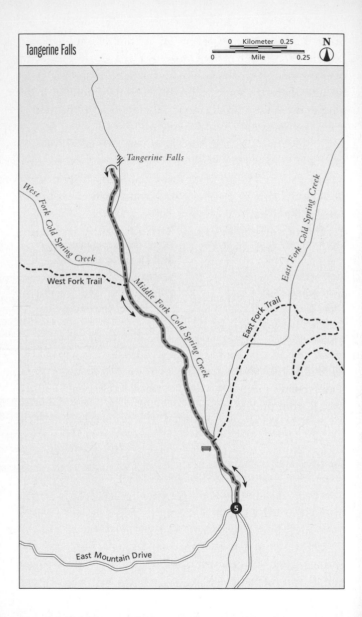

Tangerine Falls

West Fork Cold Spring Creek

West Fork Trail

Middle Fork Cold Spring Creek

East Fork Cold Spring Creek

East Fork Trail

5

East Mountain Drive

0   Kilometer   0.25

0   Mile   0.25

N

original route, it is no longer an established trail and can be somewhat difficult to follow at times. Increased usage over the years has helped form an unofficial trail. However, because there are some technical sections of boulder hopping that require coordination and a good grip, this trail is not recommended for small children.

This hike begins at the trailhead that leads to all forks of the Cold Spring Trail. You can begin the trail from either side of the creek, since both forks will merge a short ways in. Reach a fork in the creek at 0.2 mile. There is a bench here, and a metal sign on your left indicates the West Fork Trail. From here the trail branches in two main directions. The right fork (East Fork Trail) heads up the east side of the creek; the left heads up to the West Fork Trail. To continue on toward Tangerine Falls, bear left on the West Fork Trail past the metal sign and cross over the creek.

After crossing the creek, the trail begins to climb and roughly follows the creek on the west side. There is a large metal pipe in the ground running along the trail. Be careful not to trip on it—it seems to rise and fall in the most inconvenient places, making you duck under and clamber over it from time to time.

At 0.7 mile there is an unmarked fork. The trail straight ahead is the West Fork Trail and becomes a steep uphill climb to Gibralter Road. Instead take the right fork here, going past the large boulder on your right and into a creek. This creek may be dry, but the creekbed will be obvious. This first creekbed is the west fork of Cold Spring Creek. Cross the creek and climb up the embankment on the other side.

Once across, you will reach the middle fork of Cold Spring Creek. A small fork on your right leads down to the middle fork of the creek. Take the left path, which heads straight and begins to curve up a hill. The trail narrows and follows above the creek. At 0.8 mile bear right to continue following the creek. Just past this fork, cross the creek to the east side. Here the trail begins to disappear and you will have to start getting creative.

At 0.9 mile the trail heads steeply up the east side of the creek and around a tree. Just beyond this uphill the trail crosses the creek back to the west side. Follow the trail steeply up the west side of the creek, hopping over boulders and climbing around trees. Your efforts will pay off at 1.0 mile when you catch your first glimpse of the falls on your right. From here just keep making your way up toward the falls. At the giant boulder just before the falls, climb up and around to the left of the boulder and then drop back down toward the creek on your right. At 1.1 miles you can dip your feet into the pool at the bottom of the falls or, better yet, stand under them for an amazing shower.

Miles and Directions

0.0 Start at the trailhead on East Mountain Drive.

0.2 Reach the fork that separates the Cold Spring Trail-East Fork and Cold Spring Trail-West Fork. Take the left fork, go past the metal sign indicating the West Fork Trail, and cross the creek.

0.7 Bear right at an unmarked fork; go past the large boulder and into the creek. Cross the creek (this maybe a dry creek-bed).

0.8 Once across the creek, go left, heading up the hill. Shortly thereafter, arrive at a small fork. Bear right, staying close to the creek.

0.9 Cross the creek to the east side and head up the steep incline. Then cross back to the west side of the creek.

1.0 Continue straight ahead up the steep incline, staying to the left of the rocks. When you reach the large boulder just before the falls, climb up on the left side of the boulder. Once on top of the boulder, drop down around to the right.

1.1 Arrive at the base of Tangerine Falls. This is your turnaround point.

2.2 Arrive back at the trailhead.

6 Cold Spring Trail: East Fork

This creekside hike climbs up the east side of Cold Spring Canyon alongside a number of cascades, waterfalls, and swimming holes before traversing up the canyon and emerging atop the canyon ridge to sweeping views from the Montecito Overlook.

Distance: 2.6 miles out and back
Approximate hiking time: 1.5 hours
Difficulty: Moderately easy; long uphill
Trail surface: Dirt path
Best season: Year-round
Other trail users: Joggers
Canine compatibility: Dogs permitted
Fees and permits: No fees or permits required
Schedule: Anytime
Maps: USGS Carpinteria
Trail contacts: USDA Forest Service, Los Padres National Park; (805) 967-3481; Montecito Trails Foundation; (805) 568-0833

Finding the trailhead: From Santa Barbara take US 101 south toward Montecito. Exit at Hot Springs Road and turn left. Go 2.2 miles and turn left onto East Mountain Drive. Go 1.1 miles to a bend in the road where the creek runs across it. Park along the road on either side of the creek. GPS: N34 27.353' / W119 39.176'

The Hike

Cold Springs Trail is one of the area's great trails. Easily accessible from town, the trail takes you immediately into nature. After the first 0.1 mile you'll be immersed in sandstone walls, walking through groves of sycamore trees, and following Cold Spring Creek. Originally built to allow early settlers to mine for the coal and limestone found farther up

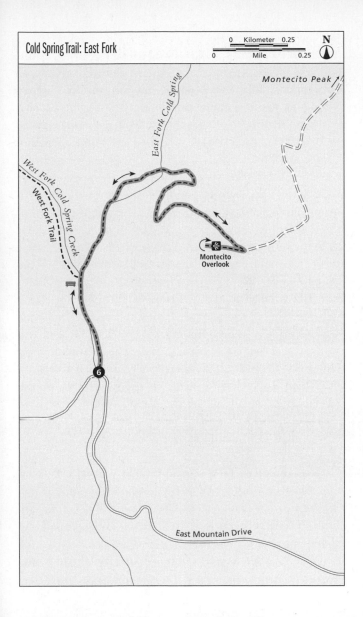

Cold Spring Trail: East Fork

0   Kilometer   0.25

0   Mile   0.25

N

Montecito Peak

East Fork Cold Spring

West Fork Cold Spring Creek

West Fork Trail

Montecito Overlook

6

East Mountain Drive

the Santa Ynez watershed, the Cold Spring Trail was one of the earliest trails built to cross the Santa Ynez Mountains. This trail greatly increased the settlers' ability to mine and find wealth and further opened up the mountain wall, connecting the town to the frontcountry.

To begin this hike, take the path on the north side of the road at the COLD SPRING TRAIL sign and continue hiking straight. At approximately 0.1 mile you will come to a fork at the creek. The left fork will lead you to the West Fork Trail. Stay to the right to continue on the East Fork Trail toward the Montecito Overlook. A bench at this junction makes a nice spot for a picnic. It's also a good turnaround point for those short on time but in need of an escape to nature. Continue past the bench as the trail follows the creek.

Begin hiking up the switchbacks through a clearing with views of the canyon, and then follow the trail back into the shade of the sycamore trees. At 0.4 mile you will come to your first creek crossing. There are plenty of pools with small falls and cascades here where you can take a dip on a warm day or have a picnic on the shore. Pick up the trail on the other side of the creek and continue past more pools and cascades. You can walk a short ways off the trail to your right to find a quiet spot. The pools get better just off the trail.

Cross the creek for a second time at 0.6 mile. Pick up the trail on the other side and take the right fork, which leads you away from the creek via switchbacks. As you climb the switchbacks, look back at the creek. In fall and winter you can see the riparian zone all the way up the mountain. Stay left as you continue up the switchbacks until you arrive at the top, where the trail intersects a dirt road at 1.25 miles. Turn right at the road and follow it for a few steps, looking for a small trail branching off on your left. Take this trail to where it ends at 1.3 miles at the Montecito Overlook. This is your turnaround for the purpose of an easy day hike. If you are in the market for an epic workout, you can continue from here all the way to Montecito Peak, another few miles up.

Miles and Directions

0.0 Start at the trailhead on either side of the creek and continue straight.

0.1 Arrive at the junction with the West Fork Trail on the left. There is a bench here beside the creek. Continue straight to follow the East Fork Trail.

0.4 Cross the creek and enjoy the pools along the creek. A few yards off the trail on your right there are many pools and cascades—a nice place for a stop.

0.6 Cross the creek a second time and take the right fork of the trail, heading southeast up the canyon away from the creek.

0.7 Arrive at a small fork. Stay left on the main trail.

0.9 Follow the switchbacks, staying to the left side of the trail. (FYI: A few small forks along the way lead off to the right. Always take the left fork.)

1.2 Arrive at a junction with a dirt road. Turn right onto the road and go approximately 50 meters until you see a small trail on your left. Take the trail on your left toward the Montecito Overlook.

1.3 Arrive at the Montecito Overlook. Turn around and head back the way you came.

2.6 Arrive back at the trailhead.

7 McMenemy Hike

This scenic lollipop hike traverses the foothills of Montecito on sections of four different trails. After crossing San Ysidro Creek, the trail climbs uphill to a lookout point at a large stone bench. A steep ascent will lead you up to the Saddlerock Trail before meeting with the Girard Trail for a long, winding downhill trek.

Distance: 4.3-mile lollipop
Approximate hiking time: 2 hours
Difficulty: Moderate; some steep uphill sections
Trail surface: Dirt trail
Best season: Year-round
Other trail users: Joggers
Canine compatibility: Dogs permitted

Fees and permits: No fees or permits required
Schedule: Anytime
Maps: USGS Carpinteria and Santa Barbara
Trail contacts: USDA Forest Service, Los Padres National Forest; (805) 967-3481; Montecito Trails Foundation; (805) 568-0833

Finding the trailhead: From downtown Santa Barbara take US 101 south toward Montecito and exit at San Ysidro Road. Turn north toward the mountains and drive 1.0 mile to East Valley Road. Turn right onto East Valley Road; drive 0.9 mile and then turn left onto Park Lane. Drive 0.4 mile to a Y in the road and take the left fork onto East Mountain Drive. Follow this road to where it dead-ends, and park along the street. The trailhead is on the right-hand side of the road. GPS: N34 26.757' / W119 37.312'

The Hike

The McMenemy hike begins at the trailhead for a number of different trail systems, all maintained by the Montecito

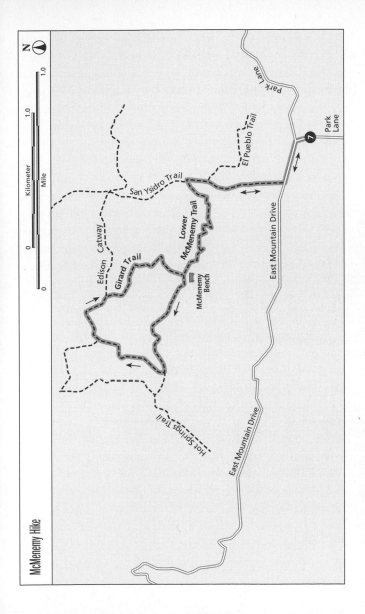

McMenemy Hike

N

Kilometer
Mile

Park Lane

El Pueblo Trail

San Ysidro Trail

Edison Catway

Girard Trail

Lower McMenemy Trail

McMenemy Bench

East Mountain Drive

Hot Springs Trail

East Mountain Drive

Park Lane

7

Trails Foundation, that you can mix and match to make a hike the length and intensity you are looking for. These trails are all marked with MTF signs, denoting that the trail has been mapped and is maintained by the foundation.

Begin this hike by heading up the trailhead alongside some private homes. After a short stretch the trail intersects a road. Turn left when you reach the road and look for the trail again on your left. Veer toward the creek and then back to meet up with the road again at 0.3 mile. The road dead-ends, but the trail continues as a dirt access road, just beyond a locked gate. Continue straight down the dirt road until you see a sign at 0.5 mile for Lower McMenemy Trail. Turn left here to follow the sign and cross San Ysidro Creek. Pick up the McMenemy Trail on your left. Continue up this gradual incline until you reach a fork at 0.6 mile. Turn right at the fork and begin a series of switchbacks up toward the McMenemy Bench.

At 1.1 miles take the left fork a short ways to a lookout point or turn right to continue on the trail. From here the trail heads west with views of the ocean. At 1.2 miles you will reach the McMenemy Bench—a large stone bench perched high atop the hill where you can relax and take in the view. This bench was made in honor of Col. Logan McMenemy, who created this trail and started the Montecito Trails Association, which became today's Montecito Trails Foundation. There is a hitching post here if you happen to have traveled here via horse. When you are at the bench facing west, you can see the junction with the Girard Trail a few yards ahead on your right. You will return via this trail, but for now continue straight down the McMenemy Trail. The trail heads downhill here for a short ways.

At 1.7 miles the trail begins switchbacking back up the hillside through a number of sandstone outcroppings. After a short climb, come to a fork at a very large tree at 1.8 miles. The left fork heads toward the Hot Springs Trail, which hikes up the next canyon over. Turn right to continue on this loop, and begin a steep ascent through boulders. This portion of the hike might resemble a step aerobics class but is well worth the effort. Stop and take a rest atop any of the large boulders, all offering incredible views, or continue huffing your way up a short ways farther. At 2.1 miles you will crest the hill and emerge onto an open landing resembling a helicopter landing zone, with a few large boulders strewn about. The trail continues ahead, just to the left and behind the largest boulder.

Continue another 0.25 mile of rolling uphill until you intersect a dirt road known as the Edison Catway. Turn right onto the road and follow it a short 0.25 mile to another junction at 2.5 miles. Turn right here onto the Girard Trail. This trail loops back toward the ocean and meets back up with the McMenemy Trail at the stone bench at 3.1 miles. From here turn left and head back down the mountain the way you came.

Miles and Directions

0.0 Start at the San Ysidro trailhead on the right side of the road.

0.1 The trail emerges onto a road. Go left and pick up the trail on the left side.

0.3 The trail again merges with the road. As the paved road dead-ends, continue straight through the locked gate.

0.5 At the sign for the Lower McMenemy Trail, turn left off the main trail onto a smaller singletrack. Cross the creek and continue left on the other side.

0.6 Arrive at a fork. The left fork leads to a gravel road. Turn right and begin switchbacks.

1.1 Arrive at a fork. The left fork leads to a viewpoint. Turn right to continue on the trail.

1.2 Reach the stone McMenemy Bench. Continue straight past the bench on your left and begin a short descent. (**Option:** This makes a good turnaround point for those looking for a short hike.)

1.3 Pass a large water tank on your left.

1.7 Begin uphill switchbacks through a maze of sandstone outcroppings.

1.8 After an uphill climb, arrive at a fork at a large tree. Turn right and continue rock hopping your way up a steep portion of the trail. (FYI: Turning left here would take you to the Hot Springs Trail.)

2.0 Arrive at a nice viewpoint.

2.1 Arrive at a flat open landing with numerous large boulders. Pick up the trail on the left side of the large boulder straight ahead.

2.2 Continue uphill, crossing under power lines.

2.3 Arrive at the junction with a dirt road—the Edison Catway—and turn right.

2.5 Head right at the fork onto the Girard Trail to wind your way back toward the ocean.

2.6 Pass the power lines again and turn right to continue down the trail.

2.9 Arrive at a fork, with a set of dirt steps to your left. Turn right to continue down the trail, and wind your way back to the junction with the McMenemy Trail.

3.1 Arrive back at the stone bench. Turn left to continue back down toward the trailhead.

4.3 Arrive back at the trailhead.

8 San Ysidro Falls

This hike takes you on a hefty uphill climb alongside San Ysidro Creek, passing a number of excellent swimming holes lined with flat rocks perfect for lounging. You can make it a short 2.0-mile hike to the best swimming hole and back or a 3.6-mile round-trip to a 60-foot waterfall.

Distance: 3.6 miles out and back to the waterfall
Approximate hiking time: 2 hours
Difficulty: More challenging; significant elevation gain
Trail surface: Dirt road, forested trail
Best season: Year-round
Other trail users: Joggers, mountain bikers on first portion

Canine compatibility: Dogs permitted
Fees and permits: No fees or permits required
Schedule: Anytime
Maps: USGS Carpinteria
Trail contacts: USDA Forest Service, Los Padres National Forest; (805) 967-3481; Montecito Trails Foundation; (805) 568-0833

Finding the trailhead: From downtown Santa Barbara take US 101 south toward Montecito and exit at San Ysidro Road. Turn north toward the mountains and drive 1.0 mile to East Valley Road. Turn right onto East Valley Road; drive 0.9 mile and turn left onto Park Lane. Drive 0.4 mile to a Y in the road and take the left fork onto East Mountain Drive. Follow this road to where it dead-ends, and park along the street. The trailhead is on the right-hand side of the road. GPS: N34 26.757' / W119 37.312'

The Hike

A short drive through one of Santa Barbara's wealthiest neighborhoods will take you to the trailhead of this creekside hike. Start the hike by walking a short ways up the

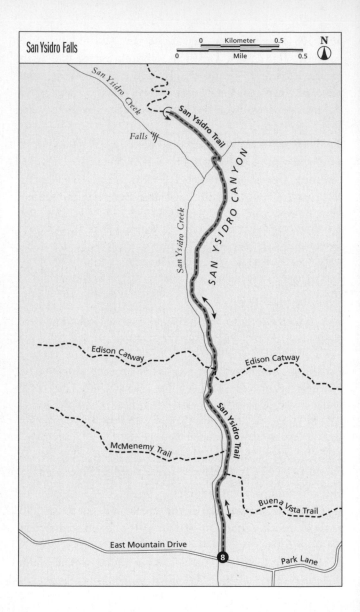

San Ysidro Falls

San Ysidro Creek

San Ysidro Trail

Falls

San Ysidro Creek

SAN YSIDRO CANYON

Edison Catway

Edison Catway

McMenemy Trail

San Ysidro Trail

Buena Vista Trail

East Mountain Drive

8

Park Lane

Kilometer

Mile

N

dirt path alongside some private homes. After 0.1 mile the trail intersects a road. Turn left and look for the trail again on the left side of the road. The trail meets back up with the road again at 0.4 mile and follows it a short ways until the road dead-ends and the trail continues, becoming a dirt access road.

Continue straight through the gate. At 0.5 mile there is a fork on your left that leads to the McMenemy Trail. To continue toward San Ysidro Falls, go straight on the dirt road. At 0.9 mile leave the main trail by taking the single-track trail on your right. This trail will begin to follow the San Ysidro Creek. The trail follows the creek for the next 0.75 mile, with a number of offshoot trails that lead down to the water. There are some great swimming holes along the way and a number of cascades and mini-falls before you reach the main falls.

On your left at 1.3 miles and again at 1.4 miles are some of the best swimming holes on the creek. Stop here for a swim or a picnic, or continue on toward the falls by heading straight up and beginning a set of steep switchbacks. The trail gets significantly steeper from here, so be prepared for a real workout once you leave the creek. There are metal railings along the switchbacks here for a short ways before the trail heads back down into the creek. Cross the creek at 1.7 miles and continue straight. You can also turn right once you cross the creek to rock hop your way up the creek to find additional swimming holes.

Continue straight across the creek and go about 100 yards to a fork. Continue straight at the fork and arrive at the waterfall a few yards ahead.

The right fork will lead you on a slippery uphill climb to East Camino Cielo. This is an excellent workout and provides rewarding views, but be prepared with plenty of water—the ridge is very exposed and steep.

Miles and Directions

0.0 Start at the trailhead on the right side of the street.

0.1 The trail intersects a road. Turn left and continue up the road, picking up the trail again on your left.

0.4 The trail merges with the road once again. The road dead-ends here. Continue on the trail through the gate.

0.5 Arrive at a junction with the McMenemy Trail on your left. Continue straight on the San Ysidro Trail.

0.6 Pass through a second gate.

0.9 Leave the main trail and take the singletrack trail on your right. Follow the trail along the creek.

1.1 Continue straight.

1.3 Arrive at an excellent swimming hole on your left. Stop here or stay straight to continue hiking toward the falls.

1.5 Continue up the steep switchbacks.

1.7 Cross the creek and take the left fork. Continue 100 yards to another fork. Stay straight to continue to the falls. (**Option:** The right fork begins a steep ascent to East Camino Cielo.)

1.8 Arrive at the falls. Turn around and retrace your steps.

3.6 Arrive back at the trailhead.

⑨ Inspiration Point

This easily accessible hike starts close to the center of town and quickly rises up a well-marked trail. It traverses through chaparral and sandstone walls before emerging atop Inspiration Point with views of Santa Barbara, the Pacific Ocean, and the coastline.

Distance: 3.6 miles out and back
Approximate hiking time: 1.5 hours
Difficulty: Moderate
Trail surface: Gravel road followed by forested trail
Best season: Year-round
Other trail users: Joggers

Canine compatibility: Dogs permitted
Fees and permits: No fees or permits required
Schedule: Anytime
Maps: USGS Santa Barbara
Trail contacts: USDA Forest Service, Los Padres National Forest; (805) 967-3481

Finding the trailhead: From downtown Santa Barbara head northeast on Mission Street past the mission to Foothill Road. Turn right onto Foothill Road; go 0.1 mile and turn left onto Mission Canyon Road. At the fork in the road at 0.2 mile, bear left onto Tunnel Road. Follow Tunnel Road 0.4 mile until it dead-ends. Park on the side of the road. GPS: N34 27.898' /W119 42.764'

The Hike

Inspiration Point is the perfect day hike from Santa Barbara if you are looking to get a lot out of a little time and energy. The hike is challenging, but at a reasonable pace you can be back to your car in an hour and a half. This hike gives you a nice, neat package of Santa Barbara hiking: quick access from town, a good workout, a taste of nature, and gorgeous views.

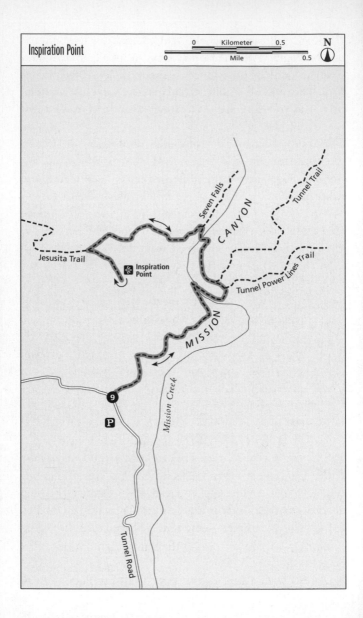

Inspiration Point

Jesusita Trail

Inspiration Point

Seven Falls

CANYON

Tunnel Trail

Tunnel Power Lines Trail

MISSION

Mission Creek

9

P

Tunnel Road

Kilometer

Mile

N

Beginning from Tunnel Road you will see the trailhead on your right. There are many ways to hike from this trailhead, so don't assume you can simply follow other hikers here. The trails off Tunnel Road connect with myriad other trails, and you can hike a substantial distance in many directions from here.

To begin the hike to Inspiration Point, pass the locked gate and head up the paved road. You will stay on this paved portion for a short while before the path segues into a dirt trail.

At 0.5 mile you will come to a fork. Stay on the wide road on the left. Continue as the trail takes you farther into the forest and crosses Mission Creek. Mission Creek flows from the mountains, down past the mission, and into the heart of town. This creek was significant because it provided the Chumash Indians with the water they needed to grow crops. When Mission Canyon was originally settled, this creek flowed year-round. Today Mission Creek usually flows only at its headwaters. There are currently a number of projects in place to restore the natural habit of Mission Creek—most notably its once-thriving population of steelhead trout.

A short ways past the creek, at 0.9 mile, is a fork. The trail to your right leads to the Tunnel Power Lines Trail. Stay to the left on Jesusita Trail to head toward Inspiration Point. Continue on this trail as it heads up into the mountains on a nice singletrack. The trail winds through the trees in and out of the shade as it gently climbs its way up. Watch out for poison oak here—the trail is littered with it. Poison oak is especially hard to see in the winter months, when the branches are bare.

At 1.0 mile a fork to the right leads up Tunnel Trail.

Bear left on the main trail and continue straight ahead. Cross Mission Creek again at 1.2 miles. Once across the creek you can take a detour and go right to rock hop up the creek to a popular area known as Seven Falls, where there are numerous cascades and swimming holes along the creek.

To continue to Inspiration Point, stay on the trail to your left. After this second creek crossing, the trail gets a bit steeper and switchbacks take you up to the top of the peak. Emerge from this climb at a road at 1.7 miles. Directly across from the road is a smaller trail that leads a short ways to a beautiful overlook. This is an excellent spot to take a rest, have a snack, and take in the views of the city below. But don't get too comfortable. Though some might argue that this point is truly inspirational, this is not the namesake Inspiration Point.

To continue to Inspiration Point, backtrack to the road and turn right. (If you were turning onto the road from the trail on the way up, you would turn left.) Head down the road a few hundred yards and look for a small trail on your right. Take this less-traveled trail and wind your way through the brush until the trail disappears at a small pile of large boulders—the true Inspiration Point. From atop these boulders you can see all the way down the California coast.

Miles and Directions

- **0.0** Start at the trailhead at the end of Tunnel Road.
- **0.5** Arrive at a fork. Stay on the main trail on the left.
- **0.9** Go left at the fork onto the Jesusita Trail.
- **1.0** At the fork in the trail, stay left to continue on the Jesusita Trail.

1.2 The trail crosses Mission Creek for a second time. Continue on the main trail on the left. (**Option:** Turn right after the creek crossing to detour to Seven Falls.)

1.7 Emerge from the chaparral onto a road. Turn left on the road to continue to Inspiration Point. (**Option:** Go straight across the road to an overlook.)

1.8 Take the small singletrack trail on your right back into the chaparral.

1.8 Arrive at the cluster of rocks that mark Inspiration Point and your turnaround.

3.6 Arrive back at the trailhead.

10 Rattlesnake Canyon

A shady refuge on a sunny day, this trail winds its way up Rattlesnake Canyon, loosely following the creek for a gradual uphill to Tin Can Meadow. From here you can take in the view and retrace your steps home or continue onto the Tunnel Connector Trail to hike into the Santa Ynez Mountains.

Distance: 3.3 miles out and back

Approximate hiking time: 1.5 hours

Difficulty: Easy to moderate

Trail surface: Forested trail, creekbed

Best season: Year-round

Other trail users: Joggers

Canine compatibility: Dogs permitted

Fees and permits: No fees or permits required

Schedule: Anytime

Maps: USGS Santa Barbara

Trail contacts: USDA Forest Service, Los Padres National Forest; (805) 967-3481

Finding the trailhead: From downtown Santa Barbara drive northwest toward the mission. Take Mission Canyon Road north toward the mountains and turn right onto Foothill Road. Drive 0.15 mile and turn left onto Mission Canyon Road. Drive 0.5 mile and turn right onto Las Canoas Road, following the signs toward Skofield Park. Drive approximately 1 mile to the stone bridge signifying the trailhead. Park along the road. GPS: N34 27.453' / W119 41.530'

The Hike

Despite the daunting name, the hike through Rattlesnake Canyon is actually quite a peaceful one. You are no more likely to see a rattlesnake here than on any other trail in the area. Rather the trail is named for its twisty and curvy

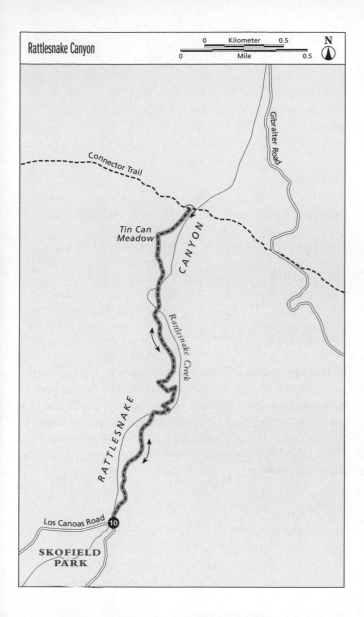

Rattlesnake Canyon

0   Kilometer   0.5

0   Mile   0.5

N

Gibralter Road

Connector Trail

Tin Can Meadow

CANYON

Rattlesnake Creek

RATTLESNAKE

Los Canoas Road   10

SKOFIELD PARK

nature, resembling a slithering snake. The canyon begins at Skofield Park, a popular location for softball games and group events, and stretches up into the Santa Ynez Mountains via the Tunnel or Gibralter Trail. Dams were built throughout this canyon in the early 1800s to aid in the efforts to bring water to Mission Canyon. Today only minimal remains of these dams survive, giving hikers the benefit of small man-made waterfalls.

To begin the hike, walk to the right of the large stone bridge and begin up the trail following along the east side of the creek. Much of the area surrounding this lower portion of the trail was burned in the Tea Fire in fall 2008, and much of the damage was still visible at the time this book was published. Fortunately the trail is still intact. The city allows hikers to pass through, despite the surrounding damage.

In the first 0.5 mile you will pass by a few small trail forks. Stay to the left, keeping close to the creek but not crossing it. At 0.5 mile cross the creek to the left and take either the right or left fork up the incline. At 0.6 mile take the right fork and then make an immediate left onto a set of switchbacks leading up and away from the creek. Continue straight, winding through a brief section of pine trees. Some say this drastic change in scenery more closely resembles a hike in the Sierras than the Santa Barbara frontcountry, but the diversity is a welcome alternative to the chaparral and sandstone borders found on many of the other hikes in this area.

At 1.2 miles cross the creek to your right. Climb over a few rocks and then cross the creek back to your left. Make a left after crossing the creek, hiking what seems to be backwards for a few yards. Bear right at the fork and continue toward Tin Can Meadow. You will reach the meadow at 1.6 miles. At the end of the meadow is a large flat rock—an excellent place for a picnic and the hike's turnaround point.

If you want to continue, a few yards beyond the meadow is a junction with the Tunnel Connector Trail and a trail that leads up to Gibralter Road.

Miles and Directions

0.0 Start at the trailhead on the east side of the stone bridge.

0.1 Arrive at a fork; stay left.

0.5 Bear left at the fork, heading toward the creek.

0.6 Cross the creek to your left. Then take the fork to your right, a trail that resembles dirt stairs. After a short ways, take the left fork. Shortly after, reach another fork and turn right followed by an immediate left, zigzagging your way away from the creek.

0.9 Continue straight ahead.

1.1 Continue straight ahead.

1.2 Cross the creek to your right. Follow the creek a short ways, and then cross the creek again, back to your left. Follow the trail along the creek a few yards before making a sharp right turn, heading back up the canyon.

1.6 Arrive at Tin Can Meadow. Retrace your steps to the trailhead. (**Option:** Continue a few yards to the junction with the Tunnel Connector Trail and access to Gibralter Road.)

3.3 Arrive back at the trailhead.

11 Santa Barbara Waterfront

Perhaps the most iconic stretch of land in all of Santa Barbara lies on the boardwalk, or beach path. This paved bike trail runs from Leadbetter Beach, past the harbor and the Santa Barbara Wharf, and ends at the beach volleyball mecca of East Beach.

Distance: 4.2 miles out and back
Approximate hiking time: 1.5 hours
Difficulty: Easy
Trail surface: Paved path
Best season: Year-round
Other trail users: Cyclists, pedicabs
Canine compatibility: Leashed
dogs permitted
Fees and permits: Parking fee may be required, depending on where and when you park.
Schedule: Anytime
Maps: USGS Santa Barbara
Trail contacts: City of Santa Barbara Parks and Recreation; (805) 564-5418

Finding the trailhead: From downtown Santa Barbara drive south toward the beach. State Street, or any street running parallel to it, will dead-end at Cabrillo Boulevard. Turn right onto Cabrillo and head west. You will pass the harbor on your left. Turn left onto Loma Alta Drive in the parking area. Park in the lot on either side of the street. GPS: N34 24.155' / W119 41.872'

The Hike

The boardwalk along the Santa Barbara waterfront can be an excellent way of getting to whichever beach you plan to spend your afternoon, or it can be a lovely walk in itself. Although the path can get crowded in summer with beachgoers and tourists riding those giant four-person beach cruisers, braving the crowd can be worth it, especially in the early

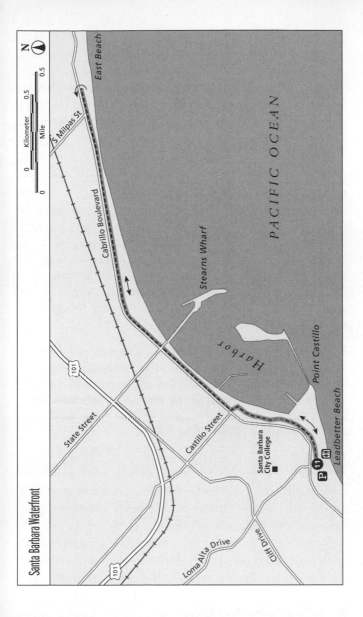

Santa Barbara Waterfront

evenings when you can watch the sunset over the wharf. This walk can be done from end to end of the boardwalk, or you can park anywhere along the way and simply stroll as long as you wish in either direction. The walk described here goes from Leadbetter to East Beach and back.

Starting from the west end, you can begin the walk at Leadbetter Beach. A popular place for surfers and kite-boarders, Leadbetter also has barbecue areas that are open to the public. From here walk east through the parking lot toward the harbor. At 0.2 mile from Leadbetter Beach you will reach Santa Barbara Harbor, where you can have your pick of seafood restaurants as well as a place to rent kayaks or buy bait.

From the harbor continue east as the marked path curves through another parking lot and out toward Cabrillo Boulevard. The path intersects Cabrillo just past the public swimming pool. From here you can follow either the sidewalk or the separate bike path. If you are traveling by foot, it might be a good idea to stick to the sidewalk to avoid having to dodge speeding cyclists or reckless surrey drivers. If you are on a bicycle, you should stick to the bike path.

After 0.9 mile you will come to Stearns Wharf. Built in 1872 to service cargo ships, the wharf has transformed into a tourist attraction that boasts a number of shops and restaurants. The wharf is also the home of the Ty Warner Sea Center, open year-round and host to the annual Santa Barbara holiday boat parade and fireworks show.

Continue past the wharf and pass a long strip of grass. On Sunday a lively arts and crafts show is set up here, with local artists selling their original paintings, ceramics, and jewelry. The fair is held every Sunday from 10:00 a.m. to sundown and also on select Saturdays and three-day weekends.

Continue past the booths and at 2.1 miles reach the bathhouse and the Cabrillo Arts Pavilion at East Beach. East Beach hosts a number of official and unofficial volleyball tournaments throughout the year. You are likely to see die-hard fans out playing in their bikinis any month of the year, regardless of the temperature. East Beach is also home to the East Beach Grill, a great place for enjoying a burger or a beer just steps from the sand.

Once you have had your fill of sand and sea, turn around here and head back the way you came. If you want to keep going, cross the street. The path continues toward the Santa Barbara Zoo and a bird refuge.

Miles and Directions

0.0   Start at the parking area at Leadbetter Beach. Walk through the parking lot, heading east.

0.2   Arrive at the harbor on your right. Continue straight through the parking lot, following the path on the right-hand side of the road. Follow the path as it curves through the harbor parking area.

0.5   Continue following the path around the public pool.

0.6   The path intersects the sidewalk on your left. Either continue on the bike path along the sand or take the parallel sidewalk.

0.9   Arrive at the wharf. Continue straight, following the path.

2.1   Arrive at East Beach, the turnaround point for this hike. (**Option:** Cross the street and pick up the path on the north side of the road to continue on toward the zoo and the bird refuge.)

4.2   Arrive back at the Leadbetter Beach parking area.

12 Douglas Family Preserve

Seventy acres of land overlooking the Pacific provide numerous options for walks and runs. The preserve can be accessed from various points and is dog friendly, with many off-leash areas. Native plants and birds add to the serenity here, making this a very special place for peaceful walks.

Distance: 1.6-mile lollipop
Approximate hiking time: 30 minutes
Difficulty: Easy
Trail surface: Dirt path
Best season: Year-round
Other trail users: Runners, cyclists
Canine compatibility: Dogs permitted; some areas off-leash (note signs)
Fees and permits: No fees or permits required
Schedule: Sunrise to 10:00 p.m.
Maps: USGS Santa Barbara
Trail contacts: Santa Barbara City Park Rangers; (805) 897-1941

Finding the trailhead: From downtown Santa Barbara take Las Positas Road toward the ocean. Turn right onto Cliff Drive and go 0.1 mile to the entrance to Arroyo Burro Beach on your left. Drive into the parking lot and turn left. Park at the east end of the lot. The trail begins at the edge of the parking lot. GPS: N34 24.276' / W119 44.458'

The Hike

The Douglas Family Preserve sits atop seventy acres of wooded land above Arroyo Burro Beach. This land, formerly known as the Wilcox property, was slated for development until the local community, with the help of celebrity Michael Douglas, stepped in to save it in 1997. Named in

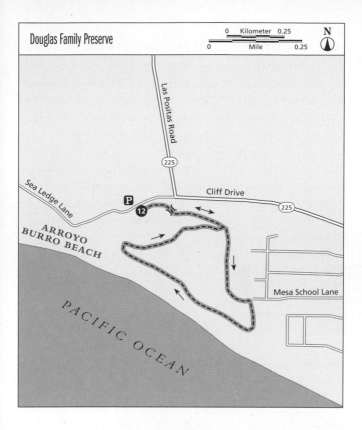

honor of Michael Douglas's father, Kirk, the Douglas Family Preserve assures that the local flora found here remains protected. The Douglas Family Preserve is open to runners, walkers, bicyclists, and dogs and contains a rare species of coastal oak tree. It is also home to the great horned owl, red-tailed hawk, and many other bird-watchers' delights.

You can access the property from a number of different places. A trail leads up from the beach below through the adjoining neighborhood known as "the Mesa" or from the parking lot of Arroyo Burro beach, as described above. A main trail loops around the perimeter of the property, with multiple offshoot trails traveling through it. Although dogs are allowed on most parts of the trail, they are prohibited from certain portions deemed "quiet areas." Signs are posted throughout the preserve to help you know when to take your dog off, or put him back on, the leash. However, it is not uncommon for a leashed dogs area to lead directly to a no dogs allowed area, which, needless to say, can be confusing.

For the lollipop hike described here, start from the parking lot and begin walking on the dirt path, following the road. This will lead you to a small bridge that will take you to the base of the preserve.

After a short 0.25 mile uphill, you will reach the top of the preserve, where you can take any number of trails to explore. Continue straight, hugging the outer edge of the preserve. After a short ways you will see the ocean in front of you. Turn right at the edge of the cliff to continue on the loop to the inside of the preserve. A left turn will take you out toward the neighborhood. Most of the off-leash dog area is to your right.

Continue ahead and at 1.0 mile you will find yourself toward the edge of the cliff, and from here there is another excellent viewpoint. Turn right and follow the edge of the cliff. Follow the trail as it curves again to the right, looking for hang gliders on your left, just inland from the preserve. Continue straight ahead and the trail will bring you back to the hill where you initially entered the preserve.

Miles and Directions

0.0 Start by taking the dirt path at the south end of the parking lot. Go straight.

0.1 Reach a small bridge on your right. Cross the bridge and continue straight ahead. The trail curves to the left and begins climbing uphill.

0.2 Continue straight at the fork to follow the perimeter of the preserve.

0.4 Continue straight.

0.5 Reach a junction with a gate straight ahead. To continue in the preserve, take the right fork. (**Option:** Continuing straight will lead you into the adjoining neighborhood.)

0.6 As you approach the cliff's edge, turn right onto the main trail.

1.0 Stop and enjoy the view at this lookout point. Follow the trail as it turns to the right and makes another right turn a few yards later.

1.3 Reach a fork. Make a sharp turn to your left to head back down toward the parking lot. (**Option:** Go straight to continue in the preserve.)

1.6 Arrive back at the parking lot.

13 Stevens Neighborhood Park

Easily accessible from the center of town, this flat and scenic trail begins at the hidden oasis of Stevens Neighborhood Park and takes you beneath sycamore canopies and through grassy meadows before connecting with a variety of trails. Many options are available here for an easy, pleasant day hike or a more challenging adventure.

Distance: 1.5 miles out and back
Approximate hiking time: 1 hour
Difficulty: Easy; flat, well-marked trail
Trail surface: Forested trail
Best season: Year-round
Other trail users: Mountain bikers
Canine compatibility: Leashed dogs permitted

Fees and permits: No fees or permits required
Schedule: 8:00 a.m. to half hour after sunset
Maps: USGS Santa Barbara
Trail contacts: Santa Barbara City Park Rangers; (805) 897-1941

Finding the trailhead: From downtown Santa Barbara take US 101 north and exit at Las Positas Road. Turn right onto Las Positas and continue straight as the road becomes San Roque Road. Drive 1.3 miles and turn left onto Calle Fresno. Go 0.1 mile and turn right onto Canon Drive. Make an immediate right into Stevens Park. GPS: N34 26.862' / W119 44.008'

The Hike

Amidst a pleasant residential area with wide streets and beautiful homes, Stevens Neighborhood Park, hidden in San Roque Canyon, provides a great opportunity to get into nature without ever leaving town. The trail begins at the end of the parking lot. Walk through the grassy park,

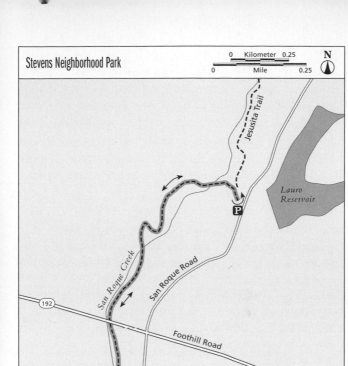

Jesusita Trail

Lauro Reservoir

San Roque Creek

San Roque Road

192

Foothill Road

192

13

past restrooms and group use areas, to the wide dirt path at the far side of the park. Once you leave the park, the trail immediately passes under the Foothill Bridge.

After the bridge the trail emerges from under the oak and sycamore trees and into a grassy meadow with views of nearby Cathedral Peak. A trail to the right will lead you back up to the road. Stay left to continue on the main trail.

The trail heads uphill slightly and then down as it comes to a creek. Cross the creek and turn left onto the trail that takes you up over the knoll. (If you go straight, you can wind your way back to the same trail, but you will encounter some overgrown sections where you may need to bushwhack.) As you go up the hill, the trail gets narrower. Emerge from the brush and head straight to cross the concrete spillway. This is another great place to take in the views of the peaks above. Continue straight through the open meadow before the trail meanders back toward the creek.

At 0.6 mile drop down and cross the creek again, picking up the trail a few strides upstream on your right. Stay straight on this trail until the fork at 0.7 mile. Here you can go right and reach a parking area on San Roque Road—your turnaround point for this hike.

Turning left will take you to the Jesusita Trail, where you can continue on a challenging hike up an alternative route to Inspiration Point.

Miles and Directions

0.0 Start at the parking lot and walk straight through the park.

0.2 Cross straight through the meadow.

0.3 Cross the creek and then turn left up over the hill.

0.5 Cross the concrete spillway and continue on the trail straight ahead.

0.6 Cross the creek again and find the trail upstream on the right.

0.7 Take the right fork up to the parking area. (**Option:** Turn left to reach the Jesusita Trail to Inspiration Point.)

0.75 Reach the parking area, your turnaround point.

1.5 Arrive back at your starting point.

14 San Antonio Creek Trail

This flat and peaceful trail begins at Tuckers Grove Park amidst baseball fields and picnic areas. It quickly leaves the crowd of the park and travels upstream along San Antonio Creek, meandering on a quiet trail through grassy meadows and under canopies of sycamore and oak trees.

Distance: 2.8 miles out and back
Approximate hiking time: 1 hour
Difficulty: Easy; flat terrain and easy-to-follow trail
Trail surface: Dirt path
Best season: Year-round
Other trail users: Bird-watchers
Canine compatibility: Leashed dogs permitted
Fees and permits: No fees or permits required
Schedule: 8:00 a.m. to sunset
Maps: USGS San Marcos Pass and Goleta
Trail contacts: Santa Barbara County Parks; (805) 568-2461

Finding the trailhead: From downtown Santa Barbara take US 101 north and exit at Turnpike Road. Turn right off the exit and go 0.7 mile to Cathedral Oaks. Cross the intersection and continue straight into Tuckers Grove Park. Turn right and drive all the way through the parking lot. Park In the last parking area in front of the locked gate at Kiwanis Meadow. GPS: N34 27.171' / W119 47.066'

The Hike

Santa Barbara County has more than twenty-three well-maintained parks sprinkled throughout the county from Santa Maria to Carpinteria. Many can be reserved for parties and events, and most have clean restrooms, picnic tables, and bars, making great destinations for a weekend outing.

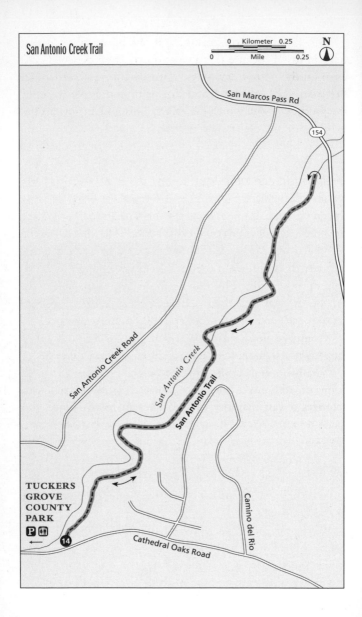

San Antonio Creek Trail

0   Kilometer   0.25

0   Mile   0.25

N

San Marcos Pass Rd

154

San Antonio Creek Road

San Antonio Creek

San Antonio Trail

TUCKERS
GROVE
COUNTY
PARK

Camino del Rio

14

Cathedral Oaks Road

The San Antonio Creek hike is one of my favorite easy trails in town because it is always quiet, often deserted, and even on the hottest days stays relatively cool in the shade of the trees. Though the destination is unimpressive in itself, the journey is well worth the effort. This hike begins off the parking lot at Tuckers Grove Park.

The trailhead is located on the left side of the parking lot, at the end of the parking spaces before the locked gate. Beginning at the TRAIL sign, follow the trail down to your left and immediately cross over the creek. At 0.1 mile cross the creek again, leading you onto the trail on the east side of the creek. Right after you cross the creek, the trail comes to a T junction at a big grassy field contained by a fence. Turn left here to continue on the trail, following along the grassy field on your right. This field is an off-leash dog park. You can bring your dogs here during specific hours as posted, generally 10:00 a.m. to noon and 4:00 p.m. to close.

Continue along this path as you wander through grassy meadows. The flora here is a bit different from other Santa Barbara hikes and can be a welcome change from the most common terrain—a hilly hike along chaparral—that char-acterizes a vast majority of the hikes in town. Enjoy the shade under the oak trees and along grassy meadows before crossing the creek at 0.8 mile and again at 0.9 mile. Just after the creek crossings, you will come to a dam. The area below the dam was badly burned during the Painted Cave Fire of 1990, but it has since been restored and reinhabited by native plants.

When you reach the dam, hike up along the right side. At the top, hike left and go over the top of the dam. Come to an intersection at 1.1 mile. Take the trail to the right and watch the scenery change from cool trees to foothill chaparral and sagebrush. Continue straight on this trail up a slight incline and veer right just before the bridge. (If you continue straight, the trail disappears beneath the CA 154 bridge.) Head up to the right; the trail ends amidst an unmonumental cluster of boulders along CA 154.

Miles and Directions

0.0 Start at the trailhead at the end of the parking lot on the left side.

0.1 Cross the creek and turn left at the T junction.

0.8 Cross the creek to your left.

0.9 Cross the creek to your right.

1.0 Arrive at the debris dam. Follow the trail up the right side. At the top, turn left and walk across the dam.

1.1 Turn right to continue on the trail.

1.4 Hike up the incline and turn right, away from the bridge.

1.4 Arrive at CA 154. Turn around here and retrace your steps.

2.8 Arrive back at the trailhead.

15 Ellwood Bluffs/Coronado Butterfly Preserve

This peaceful, shady preserve contains a large network of trails leading into one of the largest monarch butterfly preserves in California and then continuing on to beachside bluffs. Once at the bluffs, hike down to the beach for a day at one of Santa Barbara's most peaceful strips of sand.

Distance: 1.0-mile loop with longer options
Approximate hiking time: 30 minutes to 2 hours
Difficulty: Easy
Best season: Anytime; butterflies at their best from December to February
Other trail users: None

Canine compatibility: Leashed dogs permitted
Fees and permits: No fees or permits required
Schedule: Sunrise to sunset
Maps: USGS Dos Pueblos Canyon
Trail contacts: City of Goleta; (805) 961-7574; Land Trust for Santa Barbara County; (805) 966-4520

Finding the trailhead: From downtown Santa Barbara take US 101 north and exit at Storke/Glen Annie Road. Turn left off the exit and drive 0.4 mile to Hollister Avenue. Turn right on Hollister Avenue and drive 1.1 miles to Coronado Street. Turn left onto Coronado and drive 0.3 mile. You will see the beginning of the preserve on your right. Park along the street. GPS: N34 25.537' / W119 53.371'

The Hike

In this area of Ellwood there are a number of different trail systems and sights that all intertwine, making up a vast number of different ways to explore the area. One great

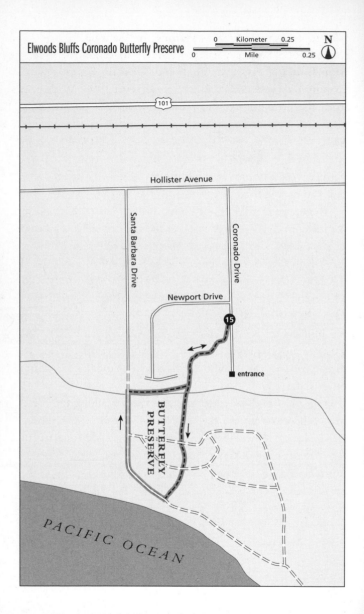

Elwoods Bluffs Coronado Butterfly Preserve

0   Kilometer   0.25
0   Mile   0.25

N

101

Hollister Avenue

Santa Barbara Drive

Coronado Drive

Newport Drive

15

entrance

BUTTERFLY PRESERVE

PACIFIC OCEAN

way to see the butterflies famous to this area, as well as the Ellwood Shores Coastal Bluffs, is to enter the Coronado Butterfly Preserve. The Land Trust for Santa Barbara County purchased this 9.2-acre preserve in 1998. With help from the community, the preserve is now a permanently protected open space where native plants like coastal sage scrub thrive. The eucalyptus groves that also have taken up residence here create the shade monarchs seek, making a perfect winter home for the butterflies, who fly up to 3,000 miles to escape the cold winters of the North.

Begin your hike by walking through the Coronado Butterfly Preserve. Small signs in the ground with a picture of a monarch stamped on them lead you through the preserve's trails. Cross Devereaux Creek, heading out toward the bluffs. Next you will come across the Ellwood Main Monarch Grove, where many miles of trail intertwine, passing the butterflies and weaving out toward the edge of the bluffs. Out by the cliff's edge is a small habitat for the western snowy plover, a sparrow-size shorebird considered threatened on the Pacific Coast and endangered in many other states.

Once at the cliffs' edge, you can traverse along the bluffs in any direction or take one of the many paths leading down to the beach. These beaches are often less populated than those closer to downtown Santa Barbara, and it wouldn't be unusual to have the beach here to yourself for a while. Take any of the many available trails back to the trailhead. Just be sure to remember which trailhead you parked your car at—the various trails lead to multiple parking areas at different ends of the preserve.

Miles and Directions

- Starting at the trailhead along Coronado Road, you will see a sign on the west side of the road introducing you to the preserve. The sign is filled with facts about the butterflies. From here you will head in toward the eucalyptus trees.

- Shortly after entering the preserve you will begin to see a number of roped-off areas indicating monarch butterfly viewing spots. From here you can hike in any direction. You can head toward the cliffs to hike down to the beach or stay on one of the many trails running parallel to the beach or zigzagging through the preserve.

- The shortest distance directly into and out of the preserve is approximately 0.5 mile out and back, although you can hike loops or figure eights up to a few miles.

16 Aliso Canyon Loop

Beginning with a 1-mile interpretive trail where you can learn about the area's flora and fauna as it pertained to the Chumash Indians, this loop trail climbs steadily through Aliso Canyon, eventually peaking just beyond a meadow. The trail then meanders down the other side of the canyon, with views of Oso Canyon to the south.

Distance: 3.4-mile loop
Approximate hiking time: 2 hours
Difficulty: Moderate; substantial elevation gain
Trail surface: Forested path
Best season: Year-round
Other trail users: None
Canine compatibility: Dogs permitted

Fees and permits: Adventure Pass required; available at the ranger station or at kiosks along Paradise Road
Schedule: Anytime
Maps: USGS San Marcos Pass
Trail contacts: USDA Forest Service, Los Padres National Forest; (805) 967-3481

Finding the trailhead: From Santa Barbara take US 101 north to CA 154. Exit at CA 154 and head north toward the mountains. Go 10.6 miles and turn right onto Paradise Road. Drive 4.5 miles and turn left at the Los Prietos Ranger Station. Follow the signs to Sage Hill Group Campground. Enter the campground and turn right. Drive to the farthest parking lot on the right. The trailhead is on the left side of the parking lot. GPS: N34 32.749' / W119 47.235'

The Hike

Aliso Canyon is a great place to view wildflowers. Though nearby Figueroa Mountain is a better known spot for wildflower enthusiasts, Aliso Canyon offers an equally impressive variety. In springtime you can see blue dicks, fairy

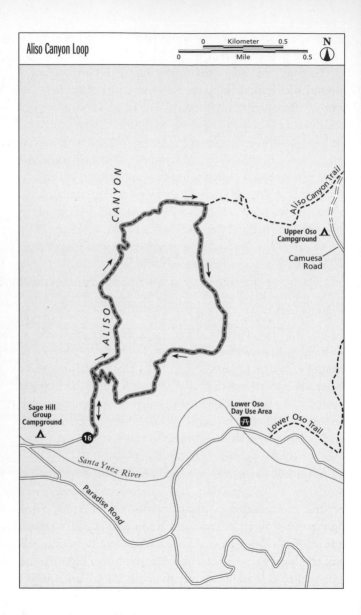

Aliso Canyon Loop

Kilometer

Mile

N

CANYON

Aliso Canyon Trail

ALISO

Upper Oso
Campground

Camuesa
Road

Sage Hill
Group
Campground

16

Lower Oso
Day Use Area

Lower Oso Trail

Santa Ynez River

Paradise Road

lanterns, and Mariposa lilies scattered along the meadows of the upper portion of trail.

To begin this hike, park in the Sage Hill Group Campground after purchasing your Adventure Pass. Although this pass is often highly disputed, if you park without buying one, you risk getting fined up to $100. If you visit here during the busy summer months, you likely won't even get a chance to park your car without a ranger or volunteer coming to your car window to sell you a day pass. Passes are available at the ranger station (if it happens to be open), from a kiosk farther down Paradise Road, or from various camp hosts strolling around the trailheads and campgrounds.

Begin at the trailhead on your left and pass the creek as you begin the interpretive portion of the trail. You can pick up an interpretation key at the ranger station that will guide you through the first mile of the trail. Numbered posts corresponding to information on your key provide information about the area. At 0.3 mile there is a fork on your right. You will return along this route, but for now continue straight. Continue to cross the creek numerous times. This is an ephemeral creek, so it could be flowing strong or entirely dry, depending on when you visit.

At 0.9 mile the trail veers sharply to the right and heads uphill. This marks the end of the interpretive portion of the trail and can be an early turnaround option.

If you choose to venture on, continue to the right and begin the steady climb up to a meadow at 1.4 miles. Just beyond the meadow is the beginning of the crest. Turn right to pass over the crest and begin heading back down into Aliso Canyon. (If you continue straight here, the trail will take you up over into Oso Canyon.) Stay right on the loop and head straight up over the peak. At 1.7 miles begin your descent back into the canyon. As you head down, be sure not to miss the views of the canyon walls behind you and look down on the Santa Ynez River below.

At 3.2 miles your downhill trail meets back up with the interpretive trail. Turn left and hike 0.25 mile back to the trailhead.

Miles and Directions

0.0 Start at the Aliso Canyon trailhead on the left side of the parking lot.

0.3 Reach a fork that intersects the return loop. Continue straight.

0.7 Follow the trail uphill, away from the creek.

0.9 Veer right up the hill and begin switchbacks.

1.4 Reach the meadow.

1.5 Arrive at a fork. Turn right to continue toward the peak. Continue straight to go up over the peak, or turn right to skirt around it—either way will lead you to the other side.

3.2 Reach the junction with the main trail and turn left.

3.4 Arrive back at the trailhead.

17 Lower Oso Trail

This relatively flat hike meanders through forested areas and meadows as it follows the path of Oso Creek. The hike climbs gently uphill, connecting the Lower Oso Day Use Area with the Upper Oso Campground. This makes for a nice stroll for those camping in the area.

Distance: 2.2 miles out and back
Approximate hiking time: 45 minutes
Difficulty: Easy
Trail surface: Forested path
Best season: Year-round
Other trail users: None
Canine compatibility: Dogs permitted

Fees and permits: Adventure Pass required; available at the ranger station or at kiosks along Paradise Road
Schedule: Anytime
Maps: USGS San Marcos Pass
Trail contacts: USDA Forest Service, Los Padres National Forest; (805) 967-3481

Finding the trailhead: From downtown Santa Barbara drive north on US 101 to CA 154. Exit onto CA 154 and drive 10.6 miles to Paradise Road. Turn right onto Paradise Road and drive 6 miles to the Lower Oso Campground. Park here and begin the hike at the junction with Romero Camuesa Road. GPS: N34 32.752' / W119 46.539'

The Hike

Beginning from the Lower Oso Campground, walk up Romero Camuesa Road. At the far end of the campground, Paradise Road continues straight toward Red Rocks. Romero Camuesa Road is the road that branches off to the left. If you were to drive up this road, it would take you up to the Upper Oso Campground.

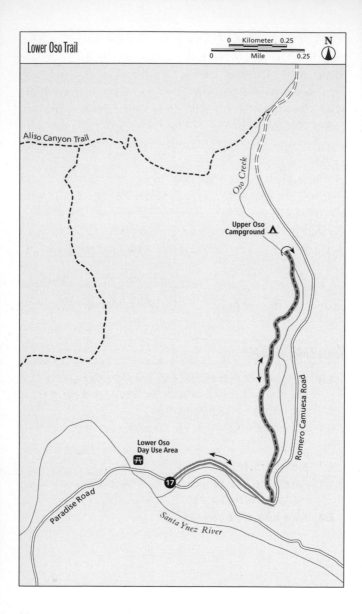

Lower Oso Trail

Aliso Canyon Trail

Oso Creek

Upper Oso Campground ▲

Romero Camuesa Road

Lower Oso Day Use Area

17

Paradise Road

Santa Ynez River

0   Kilometer   0.25
0   Mile   0.25

N

Hike up Romero Camuesa Road a short ways. At 0.3 mile cross the bridge and take the trail on the left-hand side of the road. The trail crosses Oso Creek at 0.4 mile and then meanders through meadows and trees as it gradually gains elevation. At 1.0 mile cross Oso Creek again, just before you reach the Upper Oso Campground. Upper Oso Campground begins at 1.1 miles—your turnaround point for this hike.

For a challenging hike, take the road on your left and continue up toward Little Pine Mountain or connect with the Aliso Canyon Trail. Either of these options involves a significant climb but will take you to your choice of peaks in the area. You can then connect with many trails leading into the backcountry.

The lower portion is an excellent hike if you are camping in the area with children. It makes for a peaceful walk without any difficult or strenuous terrain.

Miles and Directions

0.0 Start from the parking area at the Lower Oso Day Use area. Find Romero Camuesa Road on the left side of the parking lot and begin walking up the road.

0.3 After crossing the bridge, take the narrow trail on your left.

0.4 Cross Oso Creek.

1.0 Cross Oso Creek again.

1.1 Arrive at the base of Upper Oso Campground. Turn around here and retrace your steps.

2.2 Arrive back at the trailhead.

18 Red Rocks

This hike begins at the Red Rocks day-use area and travels in a short ways to enticing yet sometimes crowded pools with rocks for cliff jumping and rocky beaches for sunbathing. Continue past this busy college hangout a short ways and you'll find a number of options for even greater swimming holes without the crowds to contend with.

Distance: 1.0 mile out and back to main pools; 3.4 miles out and back to a more secluded pool
Approximate hiking time: 1 to 2 hours, depending on distance
Difficulty: Easy
Trail surface: Dirt road and rocky trail
Best season: Year-round. Access road to trailhead can be closed after heavy rains.
Other trail users: Mountain bikers

Canine compatibility: Dogs permitted
Fees and permits: Adventure Pass required; available at the ranger station or at kiosks along Paradise Road
Schedule: Anytime
Maps: USGS Little Pine Mountain
Trail contacts: USDA Forest Service, Los Padres National Forest; (805) 967-3481

Finding the trailhead: From downtown Santa Barbara drive north on US 101 to CA 154. Exit onto CA 154 and drive 10.6 miles to Paradise Road. Turn right onto Paradise Road and drive 10.5 miles to the Red Rocks day-use parking area. Along the way you will pass a kiosk selling Adventure Passes just before the first river crossing. Continue on and pass five additional river crossings before reaching the parking area. GPS: N34 32.107' / W118 42.708'

The Hike

A great thing about this hike is that you can make it as long

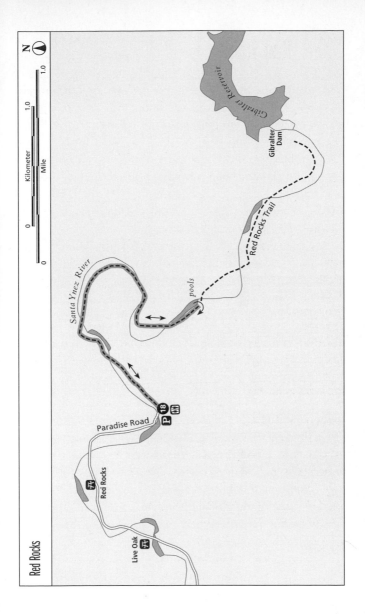

Red Rocks

N

Kilometer
0   1.0

Mile
0   1.0

Santa Ynez River

Live Oak

Red Rocks

Paradise Road

P 18

pools

Red Rocks Trail

Gibraltar Dam

Gibraltar Reservoir

or short as you want—there are perfect swimming holes along the entire trail. Whether you are looking for a rowdy pool party or a few cool laps in solitude, there is a swimming hole with your name on it at Red Rocks. The trail follows the Santa Ynez River, crossing it many times, so it is a good idea to do this hike in sport sandals or other shoes you don't mind getting wet.

Beginning from the day-use parking area, hike out on the trail just behind the restrooms. The trail begins as a dirt road traversing under oak trees until at 0.2 mile it becomes a wide cobblestone path. At 0.3 mile you come to your first of potentially many river crossings.

Just past the first river crossing, head up a short incline and drop down the other side onto the main Red Rocks pools at 0.5 mile. Here is perhaps the largest pool on the river—but also the most crowded. College students flock here on hot days, often creating an environment that more closely resembles a frat party than an escape into nature. While this pool boasts some excellent jumping rocks and good swimming, if you are looking for solitude, continue on. If you decide to swim here, use caution especially if you plan to do some cliff jumping. People can, and do, get seriously injured here. Don't assume it is safe because someone else is doing it. It isn't.

Continuing past the main pools, you will quickly see the crowd thin. Following the trail, cross the river again at 0.6 mile. At 0.7 mile the dirt road begins to disappear and you will need to follow along the rocky streambed. The road emerges again at 0.9 mile and curves around to the right as you approach another pool.

Continue walking upstream along the right bank of the Santa Ynez River. You will cross the river two more times before, at 1.7 miles, you see a shear rock face to your left. Beneath this granite wall lies a nice deep pool for swimming. This makes a good destination for a day hike. For a bigger workout, continue on this path about 2.0 miles to the Gibralter Dam.

Miles and Directions

0.0 Start at the trailhead at the Red Rocks day-use area just behind the restrooms.

0.2 The dirt road becomes a wide cobbled path.

0.3 Cross the river.

0.5 Arrive at the Red Rocks pools on the right. Stop and swim, or continue straight ahead.

0.6 Cross the river again.

0.7 The road begins to disappear. Continue straight ahead, hiking in the rocky streambed.

0.9 Pick up the road again as it turns to the right. Stop at the pool here or continue on, walking along the right bank.

1.2 Cross the river again.

1.4 Cross the river again.

1.7 Look for the deep pool beneath the shear rock face on your left. Turn around here and retrace your steps.

3.4 Arrive back at the trailhead.

19 Beach to Backcountry Trail

Amidst the rolling terrain of Gaviota State Park, the Beach to Backcountry Trail winds its way up a ridge through hillsides covered in wildflowers to large sandstone caves with views of the Pacific. After dropping down behind the caves, you will begin a short descent into a completely different environment—wooded trails hidden under heavy tree cover. Here the trail intersects a network of other trails traversing the park.

Distance: 3.4 miles out and back
Approximate hiking time: 1.5 hours
Difficulty: Moderate
Trail surface: Narrow singletrack
Best season: Year-round
Other trail users: Equestrians, cyclists

Canine compatibility: Dogs not permitted
Fees and permits: No fees or permits required
Schedule: Sunrise to sunset
Maps: USGS Gaviota
Trail contacts: Gaviota State Park; (805) 968-1033

Finding the trailhead: From downtown Santa Barbara take US 101 north approximately 32 miles to the turnoff for Gaviota State Park on the left side of the highway. Drive 0.3 mile to a fork where you see the entrance to the park on your left. Continue on the right another 0.2 mile to a dirt parking area on the right side of the road. Park here in front of the locked metal gate. GPS: N34 28.305'/ W120 13.788'

The Hike

Gaviota State Park comprises 2,775 acres of beach, trails, and campgrounds and sits a quick 30 miles up the coast from downtown Santa Barbara. The quiet beaches of Gaviota can

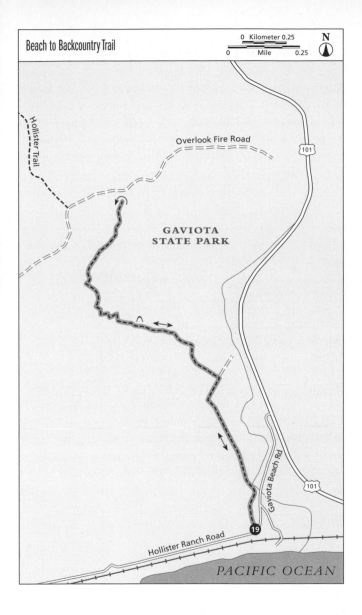

0   Kilometer 0.25

0   Mile   0.25

N

Hollister Trail

Overlook Fire Road

101

GAVIOTA
STATE PARK

19

Gaviota Beach Rd

101

Hollister Ranch Road

PACIFIC OCEAN

be a welcome change from the crowded beaches in town, but even more intriguing here are the miles of trails that are often empty. Although they aren't all as well maintained as some of the Santa Barbara frontcountry trails, the park's trails offer a great workout with even better scenery. The park is an excellent place to see wildflowers and explore sandstone caves. Part of the park lies on the east side of US 101, and the trails here lead into the Los Padres National Forest. There are also trails on the west side of the highway, creating many different possible loops.

The Beach to Backcountry Trail is just that—it begins from a dirt parking area near the beach, winds its way up a ridge, and drops you back down the other side into the backcountry. To begin this hike, walk on the gravel road just past the locked gate in the parking area. After 0.6 mile a sign on your left indicates a multiuse trail at the head of a small singletrack trail. This trail is not always well maintained and in some places may more closely resemble a game trail than a hiking trail, but it is easy to find nonetheless. Follow this trail as it winds its way steeply up the hillside. At 0.7 mile take the left fork and continue on toward a rocky ridge at 0.8 mile. Cross over the rocks and continue on through a small burn area. From between the blackened trees there are excellent views of Gaviota Peak.

At 1.0 mile pass some small caves on your left, but continue on—even better ones lie just ahead. At 1.1 miles there are some large sandstone caves on your right. After you are done exploring them, continue on the trail on the left side of the caves that takes you around behind them.

Just beyond the caves the trail begins a downhill descent. At 1.3 miles there is a brief rock scramble as the trail continues back into the canyon. At 1.7 miles the Beach to Backcountry Trail intersects the Overlook Fire Road beneath a canopy of trees. This marks a good spot to turn around.

If you want to hike farther, turn right and take the dirt road a short ways toward the radio tower. If you turn left the road intersects the Hollister Trail, taking you deeper into Gaviota State Park.

Miles and Directions

0.0 Start at the locked gate alongside the dirt parking area. Walk down the gravel road behind the gate.

0.6 Turn left at the MULTI USE TRAIL sign onto the narrow trail.

0.7 Take the left fork and continue up the hillside.

0.8 Reach the summit atop a rocky ridge.

1.0 Walk through an area of burned trees. Take in the views.

1.0 Pass caves on your left. Stay on the trail to the right of the caves.

1.1 Arrive at a small fork; stay left.

1.2 See large caves up ahead. Take the right fork to explore the caves or the left fork to continue on the hike, walking around behind the sandstone boulders.

1.3 Arrive at a small fork; continue straight.

1.7 Arrive at the intersection with the primitive Overlook Fire Road. Turn around here and head back the way you came.

3.4 Arrive back at the trailhead.

20 Gaviota Hot Springs

This short hike marks the beginning of the longer trek up Gaviota Peak. After a 0.5-mile uphill climb, you are rewarded with a small cluster of natural hot springs where you can soak your worries away in the sulfur pools. Head farther to summit 2,000-foot-high Gaviota Peak, or use this as your turnaround point for a pleasant, family-friendly hike.

Distance: 1.0 mile out and back
Approximate hiking time: 30 minutes
Difficulty: Moderate because of the short distance, but the 0.5-mile uphill trek is relatively steep
Trail surface: Dirt road, trail
Best season: Year-round
Other trail users: Mountain bikers

Canine compatibility: Leashed dogs permitted
Fees and permits: Day-use fee; fee envelopes available at the parking area
Schedule: 8:00 a.m. to sunset
Maps: USGS Solvang
Trail contacts: (805) 968-1033

Finding the trailhead: From downtown Santa Barbara drive approximately 34 miles north to CA 1. Exit at CA 1 and turn right. Take an immediate right onto the paved access road running parallel to the highway. Drive 0.3 mile to the end of the road. There is a dirt parking area here, with the trailhead and fee box on your left. GPS: N34 30.279' / W120 13.539'

The Hike

The highest peak in the area, Gaviota Peak stands at 2,458 feet, towering over Gaviota Beach below with views down the coast. The hike all the way up to the peak does offer excellent views of the area if you are up for a challenging

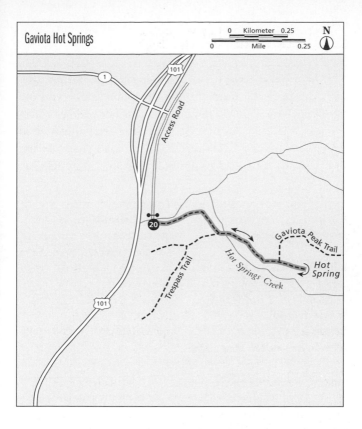

0   Kilometer   0.25   N

0   Mile   0.25

Access Road

20

Gaviota Peak Trail

Trespass Trail

Hot Springs Creek

Hot Spring

101

1

101

uphill trek. But for those looking for an easier, more family-friendly adventure, the Gaviota Hot Springs, a short ways up the trail to the peak, make a lovely destination. Begin your hike at the locked gate at the end of the parking area. Walk up the dirt road beyond the gate. At 0.2 mile the trail intersects the Tunnel View and Trespass Trail on your right. Stay left on the main trail. The road narrows and passes through sycamore groves.

At 0.4 mile the trail passes a creek. If you feel the water, you'll notice that this is actually a warm creek, running down from the hot springs above. The trail forks here. The main trail heads left and continues toward the peak. Take the trail to the right, which follows the creek for 0.1 mile before reaching the hot springs. There are three pools here, the best one being the pool on top. The temperature of the largest and warmest pool usually hovers just below 100 degrees, with the second-largest pool slightly cooler. These pools are a popular destination, so prepare for some company if you visit on weekends. Although there is supposedly a rule against nudity, it is not enforced.

Gaviota Hot Springs are sulfur hot springs, which are characterized by their rotten egg–like smell. This is caused by anaerobic bacteria living deep beneath the earth's crust. The bacteria convert dissolved sulfur in the water to hydrogen sulfide—the gas with the rotten egg odor. Although the high mineral content of hot springs are believed to have therapeutic qualities, it should be noted that these warm, moist environments also create an ideal climate for bacteria, and hazardous amoebas and other microscopic organisms can be present. These organisms work their way into your system through your mouth and nasal passages, so be sure not to dunk your head under the water and keep the water out of your nose and mouth.

Miles and Directions

0.0   Start at the trailhead behind the locked gate at the end of the parking area.

0.1   A small trail branches off to your left. Continue straight on the main trail.

0.2 Come to a sign marking the Tunnel View and Trespass Trail, which branches off to your right. Continue straight toward Gaviota Peak.

0.4 Arrive at a fork where the warm creek reaches the trail. Turn right onto a smaller trail leading to the hot springs.

0.5 Arrive at Gaviota Hot Springs, your turnaround point.

1.0 Arrive back at the trailhead.

Clubs and Trail Groups

Montecito Trails Foundation: This group monitors and maintains more than 300 miles of trails in the Montecito area. They actively work with area landowners to ensure continued access to many favorite local trails. There is a small membership fee.
P.O. Box 5481
Santa Barbara 93150
(805) 568-0833
www.montecitotrailsfoundation.org

Sierra Club of California, Los Padres Chapter: This grassroots environmental organization promotes safe and healthy use of the outdoors. Aside from lobbying environmental issues, the Sierra Club leads regular local hikes.
P.O. Box 31241
Santa Barbara 93130
(805) 965-9719
www.lospadres.sierraclub.org

Santa Barbara Mountain Trail Volunteers: This advocacy group works to build a sustainable trail system in Santa Barbara, with an emphasis on educating the mountain biking community and other trail users on safe and responsible trail sharing.
E-mail: info@sbmtv.org
www.sbmtv.org

About the Author

Bryn Fox is a freelance writer who has explored Santa Barbara County since 2001, hiking, biking, kayaking, swimming, and running. She works as a product developer making outdoor gear and lives in Carpinteria, California.

WHAT'S SO SPECIAL ABOUT UNSPOILED, NATURAL PLACES?

Beauty   Solitude   Wildness   Freedom   Quiet   Adventure
Serenity   Inspiration   Wonder   Excitement
Relaxation   Challenge

There's a lot to love about our treasured public lands, and the reasons are different for each of us. Whatever your reasons are, the national **Leave No Trace** education program will help you discover special outdoor places, enjoy them, and preserve them—today and for those who follow. By practicing and passing along these simple principles, you can help protect the special places you love from being loved to death.

THE PRINCIPLES OF **LEAVE NO TRACE**

- Plan ahead and prepare
- Travel and camp on durable surfaces
- Dispose of waste properly
- Leave what you find
- Minimize campfire impacts
- Respect wildlife
- Be considerate of other visitors

Leave No Trace is a national nonprofit organization dedicated to teaching responsible outdoor recreation skills and ethics to everyone who enjoys spending time outdoors.

To learn more or to become a member, please visit us at www.LNT.org or call (800) 332–4100.

Leave No Trace, P.O. Box 997, Boulder, CO 80306

AMERICAN HIKING SOCIETY

Because you hike.

We're with you every step of the way

American Hiking Society gives voice to the more than 75 million Americans who hike and is the only national organization that promotes and protects foot trails, the natural areas that surround them, and the hiking experience. Our work is inspiring and challenging, and is built on three pillars:

Volunteerism and Stewardship

We organize and coordinate nationally recognized programs—including Volunteer Vacations, National Trails Day ®, and the National Trails Fund— that help keep our trails open, safe, and enjoyable.

Policy and Advocacy

We work with Congress and federal agencies to ensure funding for trails, the preservation of natural areas, and the protection of the hiking experience.

Outreach and Education

We expand and support the national constituency of hikers through outreach and education as well as partnerships with other recreation and conservation organizations.

Join us in our efforts. Become an American Hiking Society member today!

American Hiking Society

1422 Fenwick Lane · Silver Spring, MD 20910 · (800) 972-8608
www.AmericanHiking.org · info@AmericanHiking.org